Alabama's Outlaw Sheriff, Stephen S. Refroe

THE LIBRARY
OF ALABAMA
CLASSICS

STEVE RENFROE
A rare image taken from the Montgomery *Daily Dispatch*, October
10, 1886

Alabama's Outlaw Sheriff Stephen S. Refroe

William Warren Rogers Sr. and Ruth Pruitt
with New Introduction by Paul Pruitt

The University of Alabama Press
Tuscaloosa

The University of Alabama Press
Tuscaloosa, Alabama 35487-0380

Published by The University of Alabama Press, 2005

∞

Library of Congress Cataloging-in-Publication Data

Rogers, William Warren, 1929–
Alabama's outlaw sheriff, Stephen S. Renfroe / William Warren Rogers and Ruth Pruitt ; with introduction by Paul Pruitt.— Rev. ed.
p. cm.
"Library of Alabama Classics."
Rev. ed. of: Stephen S. Renfroe : Alabama's outlaw sheriff. 1972.
Includes bibliographical references and index.
ISBN 0-8173-5248-1 (pbk. : alk. paper)
1. Renfroe, Stephen S., 1843–1886. 2. Sheriffs—Alabama—Biography. I. Pruitt, Ruth Rogers, 1923– II. Rogers, William Warren, 1929–Stephen S. Renfroe. III. Title.

HV7911.R46R64 2005
364.15'5'092—dc22

2004030109

Contents

For Warren and Arnold
And for Paul and Shannon

Preface

Among the villains, heroes, rogues and demigods who inhabit Southern folklore, Stephen S. Renfroe deserves a place. In the twentieth century a few popular magazine and newspaper articles have been written about Renfroe, while Carl Carmer's *Stars Fell on Alabama*, published in 1934, devoted several pages to him. Other than this, all that is known about the enigmatic sheriff who became an outlaw is in the form of legend.

In general, Renfroe appeared in the Black Belt town of Livingston, Alabama, late in the 1860's and quickly became a member of the Ku Klux Klan. He allegedly played a major role in driving out carpetbaggers and scalawags and ridding Sumter County of Radical Republican rule. After a grateful populace rewarded him with the office of sheriff, Renfroe reverted to a pattern of crime that earned him disgrace and ostracism. He became an outlaw, terrorizing the countryside and establishing a reputation as one of the South's most notorious rogues. He was, from time to time, placed in jail but always managed to escape. Renfroe's self-destructive course ended on July 13, 1886. As to his origins, his background, the details of his career—much has been speculated but little has been documented.

Renfroe's life was a tragedy, but if he was the author of his own destruction, Renfroe was as well the product of his time and place. In trying to bring Renfroe's legend to earth, the authors of this study discovered a man and his times totally inseparable. Renfroe became the personal embodiment of the acrimonious decade preceding the Civil War, the destruction of the conflict itself, and the bitter, unsettled period of Reconstruction. Although no statue commemorates Renfroe's role as a statesman, educator, or soldier (his highest military rank was that of private), a case can be made that he helped shape the course of politics in Alabama's Black Belt. Nor do the writers believe that Renfroe should be dismissed as a routine criminal undistinguished and unworthy of attention. If his historical niche is regional, Renfroe still invites study because he provides a base to document personally and generally a turbulent period in Alabama's history; because his exploits, brutal and incongruously sensitive, are inherently interesting; and because by the force of his personality, he spawned a series of legends that live on today.

To write of a man is to sit in judgment on him. Renfroe cannot return from the grave to set the record straight—for that matter, while alive he never bothered to reveal the unclear and unknown details of his life. In fact, he deliberately obscured his past. Although mistakes will appear and questions remain unanswered, the effort throughout has been to separate fact from fiction.

While in no way responsible for the study's errors, a number of people and institutions made possible the writing of this biography. Particular thanks are due Probate Judge Wilbur E. Dearman of Sumter County who willingly placed his records within easy access and contributed ideas and advice; Mrs. Nelle Stegall of Emelle, Alabama, permitted the use of her files on Sumter County; the Rev. Franklin S. Moseley of Eutaw, Alabama, kindly provided notes he had compiled on Renfroe; Milo Howard, director, and the late William Letford of the Alabama Department of Archives and History made essential research materials available. The authors are indebted to Paul Pruitt of Jacksonville, Alabama; Miriam Rogers, Kay Floyd, Carol Lauer, and Ray Granade of Tallahassee, Florida; Professors Russell Reaver and James P. Jones of Florida State University and Robert D. Ward of Georgia Southern College. All of them read the manuscript and made useful suggestions.

We wish to thank James Reese, who prepared the map of Sumter County, and Kathy Jackson Willis, Terrie Thompson, and Sarah Stapleton who typed various drafts of the study. A special word of gratitude is due Alice Nolan who designed the dust jacket. Of generous assistance were the library staffs at Florida State University, the University of Alabama, and Auburn University. Equally helpful were the staffs of the public libraries at Livingston, Mobile, and New Orleans. Courtesy and aid were extended by the National Archives and the Georgia Department of Archives and History and by officials in the courthouses of Butler, Lowndes, and Sumter Counties in Alabama and Lauderdale County in Mississippi.

William Warren Rogers, Tallahassee
Ruth Pruitt, Jacksonville

Renfroe Reconsidered
A New Introduction to Alabama's Outlaw Sheriff*

I n the spring of 1939, the Alabama folklorist Ruby Pickens Tartt visited the house of General Greenlee, an African American citizen of Sumter County. Greenlee began to tell her tales of the Ku Klux Klan and Steve Renfroe. He knew, he assured her, that the Klan's activities were wrong. But he relished telling how he would go along to hold the horses when Renfroe and other Klansmen rode from Moscow, in southwest Sumter County, to Livingston, the county seat. Greenlee knew Steve Renfroe perfectly well during those years, and recalled that he was a nice gentleman before he turned to horse-thieving and murder.[1] Old men may forget; but for Greenlee, all would be forgotten before he ceased reliving the days of his youth. If nothing else, his memories are a good introduction to the contradictions of Steve Renfroe's life.

---

* This essay is dedicated to the memory of Ruth Rogers Pruitt, Nelle Lehman Bare, and Juliet Lehman Hunter. Thanks to Juliet Rogers Pruitt, Mary Ruth Pruitt, Juliet Bare Pruitt, Paul M. Pruitt Sr., Shannon Pruitt, and Warren Rogers for assistance, discussion, and readings.

1. Ruby Pickens Tartt, "On de White Folks Side," interview with General Greenlee, Moscow, Alabama, Sumter County [dated 4/6/39], 2; copy on file in Bounds Law Library, The University of Alabama. For original see Series 15: Recollections of Post-Slavery Times (Box 11, Folder Q-6) Ruby Pickens Tartt Collection, University of West Alabama.

Brief narrative of Renfroe's life

The son of an obscure family of middling farmers, Stephen
S. Renfroe (1843-1886) returned from Confederate service to
Butler County, Alabama. There, in July 1867, he killed his
brother-in-law after a quarrel over the family's chickens. He
fled, fearing trial by a military tribunal, but such was the
disordered nature of government at the time that he was not
put on trial.[2] By 1868 Renfroe had settled in the Black Belt,
in Sumter County. He was a man of considerable charm,
intelligence, and ambition whose physical presence—he was
athletic and quietly assured—marked him as a leader. When
he was thinking clearly, Renfroe desired a conventionally
successful life. Yet for all his gentlemanly airs he was cursed
with a violent streak and an incurable taste for risk-taking.

In the Black Belt his particular combination of charm and
ruthlessness worked to his advantage, as he took a leading
part in white resistance to Republican Reconstruction.
There seems little doubt that he was a leader of the Ku Klux
Klan and a master of its night-riding technique. This tactic,
as sketched out by General Greenlee and others, involved
assembling a force some distance from the intended victims,
moving in on the target by nightfall, and then melting
away—initially in a misleading direction.[3] In addition,
Renfroe led Klan forces in at least one major riot, in March
1871 in Meridian, Mississippi. He was furthermore accused
of involvement in three daylight murders—of two freedmen
in 1869 and of a white Republican politician in 1874.[4]
These activities helped defeat Reconstruction in Alabama.

2. A letter found by William Warren Rogers Jr. indicates that the charges may
have been dropped. See Chilton and Thorington to Governor Robert M. Patton,
August 10, 1867, in the Robert Miller Patton Papers, Alabama State Department of
Archives and History.

3. For comments by Sumter County lawyer Turner Reavis on this type of
raiding, see *Testimony Taken by the Joint Select Committee to Inquire into the
Condition of Affairs in the Late Insurrectionary States: Alabama* (Washington
Government Printing Office, 1872), I: 332–333, 340, 345–346, 352 (hereinafter
Alabama Testimony, I).

4. For the proceedings against Renfroe in connection with the murder of
Republican activist Walter P. Billings, see this volume, 45–78, 88–90.

Following the state's "Redemption," Renfroe emerged as an admired farmer and politician in Sumter County.

Elected sheriff in 1877, Renfroe served for three years, his tenure marked both by acts of casual heroism in law enforcement and by astonishing violations of law—including arson, assault, burglary (twice of his own office), and blackmail. Arrested in 1880, he escaped from jail and left the state to live as an outlaw, initially with the Harrison gang in Mississippi and Louisiana. By January of 1883 he was back in Sumter County, moving in and out of Livingston, the county seat, in attempts to see his wife and son.[5] The following year he surrendered, an action he evidently came to regret, since he soon attempted another escape and was transferred to a stronger jail in Tuscaloosa. He escaped from that jail in July 1884 by burning himself out, and made his way to Louisiana, where a year later he was captured. After some unsuccessful attempts to break out of jail, Renfroe pleaded guilty in August 1885 to horse stealing and embezzlement. He was sentenced to five years and, seemingly penitent, sent to the convict labor camps at Pratt Mines near Birmingham.

In October, Renfroe escaped from Pratt Mines with three other convicts. Two of his comrades were speedily recaptured, but the wily Renfroe made his way back to his familiar haunts in the Flat Woods along the Alabama-Mississippi border. Mesmerized by the scene of his former success, he kept an eye on Livingston and made his living stealing horses. He had given up all thought of reform and had no intention of leaving the area, in spite of appeals by his remaining friends. By this time Renfroe's reputation had grown to mythic proportions, his deeds celebrated in fireside stories. Yet his fame and the rewards offered for him made him all the more vulnerable—as did the fear that he might tell what he knew about former members of the Ku Klux Klan.

5. Renfroe's first wife died in 1868; he married again in 1869 and, on the death of his second wife, for a third time in 1871. The son was the product of this last marriage. Renfroe's Sumter County wives, Mary M. Sledge and Cherry V. Reynolds, were women of property. See this volume, 6, 12–13.

In July 1886, the outlaw sheriff was taken in Mississippi and returned to Livingston. Renfroe and many of the townsfolk expected that he would be lynched; they were right. On the night of July 13, he was removed from jail and hung from a tree on the bank of the nearby Sucarnatchie River. His killers were never prosecuted.

The Rogers and Pruitt biography and its reception

The original work, *Stephen S. Renfroe, Alabama's Outlaw Sheriff,* was the product of a collaboration that spanned the years from 1963 to 1972. William Warren Rogers and Ruth Rogers Pruitt[6] realized that Renfroe's life was fascinating, tragic, and difficult to trace. The history of Reconstruction-era political violence is notoriously murky, since men like Renfroe were seldom brought to justice for their crimes. Court records were few, and neither Klansmen nor lynch mobs kept minutes. The authors persevered, however, and put together a narrative based on newspaper files, courthouse research in Alabama and Mississippi, and interviews with Livingston historians and folklorists, including at least one remarkable session with Mrs. Temple Scruggs Ennis, who as a young girl had witnessed Renfroe's killers marching him to execution.

Renfroe is in many respects a deliberately uninterpretive book, one that sought to counteract the mythologizing that had marked popular accounts of Renfroe—notably that contained in Carl Carmer's widely read *Stars Fell on Alabama.*[7] Rogers, for his part, is a historical exponent of letting facts speak for themselves. Pruitt, who considered

6. Born in 1929 in Sandy Ridge, Alabama, William Warren Rogers was educated at Auburn University and at the University of North Carolina. A student of Fletcher M. Green, he received his Ph.D. from Chapel Hill in 1959. For almost four decades he taught in the history department of the Florida State University, winning several awards for excellence in teaching and establishing himself as a prolific scholar, author, and publisher. Rogers retired from Florida State in 1996. Ruth Rogers Pruitt was born in 1921 in Fort Deposit, Alabama. Educated at Huntingdon College, Judson College, Jacksonville State University, and Florida State University, she taught English for Jacksonville State from 1962 through 1974. She died in 1996.

Renfroe a fitting subject for fiction,[8] sought to avoid what she would have considered novelistic writing. Both were aware of historic events unfolding in the Alabama Black Belt even as they conducted their research. Both spoke of that time as a second Reconstruction, a great turning point whose effects could not easily be foreseen.[9] Therefore they were determined to bring scholarly detachment to their telling of Renfroe's story—a story that was utterly relevant to the ongoing themes of public life in Alabama.

Renfroe received three principal reviews. Writing in the *Alabama Historical Quarterly,* Sarah Wiggins described the book as "a classic example that truth continues to be stranger than fiction." She praised *Renfroe's* excellent documentation in a "virgin area" of Alabama history and singled out Rogers for telling a story in a scholarly manner without "squash[ing] the life out of it."[10] Allen J. Going's review in the *Journal of American History* praised Rogers and Pruitt for their diligent research and noted that *Renfroe* "poses some interesting questions concerning lawlessness and political activities." He took the authors to task, however, for not offering "some broader interpretations of their character's significance for his time."[11]

Renfroe's third reviewer, Cody Hall of the Anniston *Star,* was perhaps the most perceptive of all. Describing Stephen Renfroe as "deeply involved in the murderous savagery of the

7. Carl Carmer, *Stars Fell on Alabama* [reprint of 1934 edition, with new introduction by J. Wayne Flynt] (Tuscaloosa: The University of Alabama Press, 1985), 126–133. The passage begins: "Steve Renfroe rode a milk-white horse into Livingston."

8. Twenty years later, she would publish a novel based on Renfroe's life. See Ruth Rogers Pruitt, *Wind Along the Waste* (Tuscaloosa: Arcadia Press, 1991).

9. The author well remembers, from the spring of 1964, sitting in a window on the second-floor of an old-fashioned drummer's hotel in Livingston, looking out on the town while the grown-ups mapped out their research and discussed, intermittently, protest marches and looming changes. From that vantage, the connection between future and past was clear enough.

10. Sara Wiggins' review can be found at *Alabama Historical Quarterly,* 34 (Summer 1972), 171–172. See also a review by W. Stanley Hoole at *Alabama Review,* 26 (January 1973), 74.

11. For Allen J. Going's review, see *Journal of American History,* 60 (March 1974), 1140–1141.

times," Hall described the white community of Reconstruction
as an "inverted society" in which "infamy became fame."
He noted that the authors had "recreated a picture of the
man and the times which grasped each other."[12] The heir
of a great family tradition of journalism,[13] Hall was better
equipped than most to understand that Renfroe's career was
not an isolated phenomenon.

Scholarly Contexts, New Discoveries

Lawbreakers like Renfroe remain enigmas. Yet human life
in the aggregate (as advanced thinkers of his time were
beginning to conclude) can be measured and comprehended.[14]
Surveying the period from the establishment of Radical rule
in 1867 to the end of Redemption in the late 1870s, historians
have been able to suggest a variety of explanations for the
activities of Klansmen. In the process they have demolished
the early testimony of white conservatives to the effect that
the Klan did not exist, that it was a political bugaboo of
Republicans—or alternately, or that its raids were nothing
more than private crimes carried out by "a few desperate,
drunken, obscure individuals."[15]

Attentive scholars from Walter L. Fleming to the present
day have confirmed that leaders of the Klan included
prominent citizens, and that its motivation was in part
ideological, a determined assertion of "White Supremacy"
and an effort to preserve the pre-war regime of race-based
labor control. The political aspect of these desires was played
out in an implacable opposition to the Republican Party and
its adjuncts, including the Union League. To achieve their
goals, Klansmen employed methods that were self-consciously

12. Quotes from Hall's review are taken from an undated clipping, circa 1972, in
possession of the author.
13. See Daniel Webster Hollis, *An Alabama Newspaper Tradition: Grover C. Hall
and the Hall Family* (Tuscaloosa: The University of Alabama Press, 1983).
14. For just this point in a crime novel of the period, see Arthur Conan Doyle,
Sherlock Holmes: The Complete Novels and Stories (New York: Bantam Classics,
1986), I: 202 [from *The Sign of Four* (1890), paraphrasing Winwood Reade, *The
Martyrdom of Man* (1872)].
15. *Alabama Testimony*, I: 344, 348 (quoted passages); see also 331, 332, 336.

revolutionary.[16] Contemporary observer Albion W. Tourgee referred to the Klan movement as a revolution, and viewed it as more than an assault on blacks and Republicans; it was rather a blow against "the Nation which had given the victim citizenship and power."[17]

Klansmen greatly benefited from the institutional weaknesses of Reconstruction-era governments, which were incapable of suppressing the endemic violence of the time, a violence that could erupt over a word, gesture, or rumor— and that could quickly escalate into mob incidents, pitched battles even.[18] Yet for all that they exploited postwar chaos, Renfroe and his counterparts were also the effective heirs of such former institutions as the slave patrol. The latter had taught young white men the discipline of night patrols and reinforced in them the antebellum tendency to view African American assemblies as evidence of conspiracy.[19] Ruthless

16. See Walter L. Fleming, *Civil War and Reconstruction in Alabama* (New York: Columbia University Press, 1905), 653–669; W. E. B. DuBois, *Black Reconstruction in America, 1860–1880* (New York: Atheneum, 1970 [1935]), 674–686; Allen W. Trelease, *White Terror: The Ku Klux Klan Conspiracy and Southern Reconstruction* (New York: Harper & Row, 1971), xi-xiii, xv-xlviii; Sarah Woolfolk Wiggins, *The Scalawag in Alabama Politics, 1865–1881* (Tuscaloosa: The University of Alabama Press, 1991 [1977], 40–41, 58–60, 69–71; George C. Rable, *But There Was No Peace: The Role of Violence in the Politics of Reconstruction* (Athens: University of Georgia Press, 1984), 81–100, 185–190; Eric Foner, *Reconstruction: America's Unfinished Revolution, 1863–1877* (New York: Harper and Row, 1988), 425–444; Michael W. Fitzgerald, *The Union League Movement in the Deep South: Politics and Agricultural Change During Reconstruction* (Baton Rouge: Louisiana State University Press, 1989), 83–84, 213–233; and William Warren Rogers Jr., *Black Belt Scalawag: Charles Hays and the Southern Republicans in the Era of Reconstruction* (Athens: University of Georgia Press, 1993), 28–30, 63–65, 80–81, 84–85, 88–89, 103–104, 105–120, 136–138.

17. Albion W. Tourgee, *A Fool's Errand: A Novel of the South During Reconstruction* (New York: Harper Torchbooks, 1961 [1879]), 254.

18. For a representative example of sudden violence (near the Georgia-Alabama border), see Sidney Andrews, *The South since the War: As Shown by Fourteen Weeks of Travel and Observation* (Boston: Houghton Mifflin Company, 1971 [1866]), 288–300.

19. Sally E. Hadden, *Slave Patrols: Law and Violence in Virginia and the Carolinas* (Cambridge: Harvard University Press, 2001), 203–220; Trelease, *White Terror,* xvii, xix, xxi-xxii; and Fleming, *Civil War and Reconstruction in Alabama,* 657–658, noting that, in the time of disorder following the war, "[t]he minds of all men turned at once to the old antebellum neighborhood police patrol."

and well-trained, Klansmen mocked authority while the shapers of native white opinion, even those who abhorred their methods, did nothing to stop them. "The revolution had been inaugurated," wrote Tourgee, adding "it was only a matter of time as to its absolute and universal success."[20]

During Reconstruction, then, Renfroe was both an outlaw and a revolutionary. Afterward he was never able to recover his equilibrium, and whatever his personal failings there can be little doubt that he was affected by problems common among Civil War survivors—specifically, by variants of what would today be called post-traumatic stress. Even men familiar with the institutionalized violence of the antebellum south were unprepared for the disorienting gruesomeness of battle, which Renfroe experienced in full at Yorktown and Williamsburg, Seven Pines, Gaines Mill (where he was wounded), and Fredericksburg.[21] A scholar of warfare has noted that combat is "a shocking, horrific and wrenching experience, which may lead to a kind of alienation from all that is normal, civil, and decent."[22] Probably, men like Renfroe never completely "returned" from the war. In any case the post-war south offered them both opportunities and rewards for indulging their worst inclinations.

Stress is more debilitating, morally and physically, when mixed with alcohol. Reconstruction-era southerners were notorious for drinking too often and too much; indeed a great deal of the violence and cruelty of the late nineteenth-century south was carried out in an alcoholic haze.[23] Renfroe himself

---

20. Tourgee, *Fool's Errand*, 258.
21. See this volume, page 5. In this connection it is interesting to note that Renfroe, though clearly no coward, deserted from the Army of Northern Virginia in January 1864.
22. Eric T. Dean Jr., "'The Awful Shock and Rage of Battle': Rethinking the Meaning and Consequences of Combat in the American Civil War," *War in History*, 8 (2001), 149–165, quoted passage on 154.
23. On heavy drinking generally, see Gaines M. Foster, *Ghosts of the Confederacy: Defeat, the Lost Cause, and the Emergence of the New South* (New York: Oxford University Press, 1987), 17–18; see also Andrews, *The South since the War*, 376–377. For good quotes on the lack of temperance in Reconstruction-era Alabama, see James B. Sellers, *The Prohibition Movement in Alabama, 1702–1943* (Chapel Hill: University of North Carolina Press, 1943), 48–49.

was reported as saying late in his career that drink had been his undoing,[24] and his case was by no means unique. The recently discovered diary of Sumter County merchant and planter T. K. Jackson reveals a similar pattern of events in the life of Jackson's father-in-law, Turner Reavis, a former circuit judge and state senator. Superficially Reavis was well-established, honored, and pacific—everything Renfroe was not. Yet as tensions along the Alabama-Mississippi border mounted prior to the Meridian riot of March 1871, Reavis resumed an old drinking habit. To Jackson's disgust, Reavis was found in Meridian shortly after the violence was ended, drunk. Ivy, possibly a former slave, fetched him home; some days later he was still "maudlin and intractable."[25]

After Reconstruction, Renfroe was much the same man; but he was of much less use to the men who had formerly excused his crimes. Now a network of planters and merchants managed a Black Belt regime based on sharecropping and crop liens. Staunch Democrats, they were allied politically with their hill country counterparts and with a growing number of industrialists in Birmingham and other cities.[26] These "Bourbon" leaders were mostly former Confederates, many of whom had supported the Klan or even ridden with

24. See this volume, pages 105, 127, and index.
25. See T. K. Jackson Diary, Turner Reavis Collection, Bounds Law Library, University of Alabama, entries for February 19, 26, March 2, 5, 8, 11, and 13, 1871. A widower, Reavis recovered from his alcoholic bout, remarried, and testified before Congress' Ku Klux Klan committee in the summer of 1871; he died the following year. See David I. Durham, "Thomas K. Jackson-Turner Reavis Notebook: Background," forthcoming in Paul M. Pruitt Jr., David I. Durham, Tony Allan Freyer, and Timothy W. Dixon, *Commonplace Books of Law: Excerpts from Law-Related Notebooks from the Seventeenth to the Mid-Twentieth Century* (Tuscaloosa: The University of Alabama School of Law, 2005). It is possible that "Ivy" was the same person as Thomas L. Ivey, a redoubtable but controversial leader of Sumter County African Americans, assassinated in 1874; see this volume, 49–51.
26. See Edward Ayers, *The Promise of the New South: Life After Reconstruction* (New York: Oxford University Press, 1992); Allen J. Going, *Bourbon Democracy in Alabama, 1874–1890* (Tuscaloosa: The University of Alabama Press, 1992 [1951]); and Jonathan M. Wiener, *Social Origins of the New South: Alabama, 1860–1895* (Baton Rouge: Louisiana State University Press, 1978).

it.[27] Unlike Renfroe or Reavis, they were men who had maintained self-control. They were willing to countenance mob violence, especially against independent-minded black men,[28] though they preferred to deal with routine cases of criminality or rebellion through the state's convict system.[29] When ordinary repression did not work with Renfroe, he became a belated proof of the adage that revolutions eat their young.

Hanging from a tree limb on the bank of the Sucarnatchie, Renfroe ceased to trouble the good people of Sumter County. Yet his death only enhanced his status as literary figure and legend. His name, like that of the greater icon Jessie James, has survived because of our love affair with outlaws, a fixation firmly established by the late nineteenth century when the frontier was closing and the forces of conformity were triumphant. Renfroe likewise holds an abiding interest for readers who recognize in him the type of outsider, familiar in characters from Othello to Jay Gatsby, who achieves high status but is doomed by self-destructive behavior and by the defense mechanisms of society. Fittingly enough, Tourgee anticipated Renfroe's fate in a fictional conversation between white southerners. These men support the Klan but recognize that "in so doing we are merely putting power in the hands of its worst elements, against whom we shall have to rebel sooner or later."[30]

27. For a fine example of a New South industrialist who recalled (with as much enthusiasm but less candor than General Greenlee) the time when he was "very nearly a Klansman," see Braxton Bragg Comer to Oscar W. Underwood, May 6, 1924 (carbon copy), in the Braxton Bragg Comer Papers, Southern Historical Collection, University of North Carolina. Comer claimed that he was indicted three times for "certain conduct" in 1874.
28. See William Warren Rogers and Robert David Ward, *August Reckoning: Jack Turner and Racism in Post Civil War Alabama* (Tuscaloosa: The University of Alabama Press, 2004 [1973]).
29. Mary Ellen Curtin, *Black Prisoners and Their World: Alabama, 1865–1900* (Charlottesville: University of Virginia Press, 2000); and Paul M. Pruitt Jr., "The Trouble They Saw: Approaches to the History of the Convict Lease System," *Reviews in American History*, 29 (2001), 395–402.
30. Tourgee, *Fool's Errand*, 292.

Though knowledge of his life and death remains incomplete, Renfroe's story sheds light on some intriguing problems. First, it suggests the social mobility open to a bold Klansman.[31] Next, it shows the extreme limits of tolerance for deviance from social norms—since Renfroe wasn't lynched until it was clear that he would neither reform nor leave.[32] Finally, scholars would do well to explore a suggestion advanced by Rogers and Pruitt, and by Carmer, that Renfroe was admired and befriended by African Americans.[33] Were Renfroe's black allies motivated by terror, by sympathy for a man in trouble, or by some other factor? One recent study indicates hitherto unexplored perceptions of kinship and obligation between some freedmen and their former owners.[34] Such a web of community was wide enough, at one point, to include Renfroe and General Greenlee. Perhaps by tracking first-hand accounts and fleeting memories, we can determine just how far it extended.

Paul M. Pruitt Jr.
Bounds Law Library
The University of Alabama

31. Michael W. Fitzgerald's recent study of Hale County suggests considerable tensions between the planter oligarchy and the instigators of the Ku Klux Klan. See his "Extralegal Violence and the Planter Class: The Ku Klux Klan in the Alabama Black Belt During Reconstruction," in Christopher Waldrep and Donald G. Nieman, eds., *Local Matters: Race, Crime, and Justice in the Nineteenth-Century South* (Athens: University of Georgia Press, 2001), 155–171.
32. It might be useful in this connection to compare what can be known of the Reconstruction-era Klan with the early history of other criminal organizations that have been hidden in plain sight. See, for example, Henner Hess, *Mafia and Mafiosi: The Structure of Power* (Lexington, Mass.: Lexington Books, 1973), 14–33, 43–73, and Letizia Paoli, *Mafia Brotherhoods: Organized Crime, Italian Style* (New York: Oxford University Press, 2003), 16–19, 33–40.
33. See this volume, 104, and see index; see also Carmer, *Stars Fell on Alabama*, 128.
34. Dylan C. Penningroth, *The Claims of Kinfolk: African American Property and Community in the Nineteenth Century South* (Chapel Hill: University of North Carolina, 2003).

Alabama's Outlaw Sheriff, Stephen S. Refroe

CHAPTER I

From Birth to Young Manhood

S tephen S. Renfroe became a man during the holocaust of Civil War. The remainder of his relatively short life was spent on the fringes or, more often, in the midst of violence. A man of many contradictions, Renfroe impressed those who knew him with his animal grace, his pride, and his vitality. If his temper sometimes flared beyond control, Renfroe was also known for his generosity, and he commanded a lasting loyalty from his friends. His looks complemented his personality. An acquaintance who knew Renfroe as a man wrote that "Physically he was a handsome, magnificent specimen—over six feet high, 200 pounds weight, athletic build, powerfully muscled, active as a cat." His grey eyes dominated a face which "seemed to indicate a vicious disposition." Yet Renfroe had an outgoing personality and possessed a "positive degree of magnetism." [1]

Another observer who hated Renfroe wrote that he was "a large, handsomely-formed man, but with a low over-reaching brow, and a movement like that of a panther." His critic quoted a remark from a man who saw Renfroe for the first time: "I never seen a puttier built man, but he's got the face of a cur on him, I'll be blamed if he aint."[2]

[1] Frank Herr, "Incidents of Reconstruction Days: Sumter County Alabama Following the Civil War," 8; ms. on file at the Sumter County Courthouse, Livingston.
[2] "Curtis," writing in Chicago *Inter Ocean*, October 9, 1874.

Renfroe's life began in Georgia in 1843. He was the oldest of seven children born to J. G. Renfroe, a native of Georgia, and M. A. P. Renfroe, his mother—a native of South Carolina. Like many of his neighbors, the elder Renfroe gathered his family and such belongings as he had and sometime in 1852 or 1853 crossed the Chattahoochee River seeking a home and fortune in the cotton lands of Alabama.

The family settled in Butler County, a red clay region about forty miles south of the state capital at Montgomery. This area, primarily agricultural, was not quite so rich as the lands of the Black Belt (located just to the north) but more fertile than the piney woods and wiregrass tracts that lay between it and the Gulf Coast. The Renfroes homesteaded in a farming community known for taxing and election purposes as "South Butler." Never achieving the status of a planter, Renfroe became a yeoman farmer whose real estate was valued in 1860 at $2,422. His personal estate was a modest $200.[3]

Growing up in the two stormy decades that preceded the Civil War, young Renfroe was the product of a land and society not far removed from the frontier yet sophisticated in many ways. His education, if sporadic and limited, made a lasting impression, for Renfroe was never a poor white, crude and unlettered. Later he developed a lucid, even graceful, writing style. Undoubtedly he was more concerned with hunting and fishing than arguments about states' rights or the abstract principles of slavery existing in the territories. But he was swayed by the magic names and oratory of Southern secessionists. William Lowndes Yancey, fire-eater without peer, was an Alabamian, and Thomas Hill Watts, the state's Civil War governor, was from Butler County.

Once secession was accomplished, raw recruits—youthful, awkward, but confident—formed themselves into volunteer

[3] Ms. Census for Butler County, Alabama, 1860, 163; on file at the Department of Archives and History, Montgomery, Alabama. On the basis of census data, newspaper accounts, and various records it seems probable beyond reasonable doubt that these are the correct origins of Renfroe, although he never revealed his early life other than in vague terms. See also Ms. Census for Sumter County, Alabama, 1870, 258; 1880, 401; on file at the Department of Archives and History.

companies. The pleasures of field and stream suddenly seemed tame compared with the exciting game of war. Young men gathered at the county seat of Greenville to offer their services to the Confederate government, and from there, one by one, the companies left for the front. Watching the clumsy tread of militia companies learning to drill, Renfroe determined to enlist. Renfroe was eighteen years old when he went to Greenville to join Captain E. Y. Hill's Jeff Davis Rangers on June 6, 1861. Arriving in Virginia, the Jeff Davis Rangers became Company G of the Ninth Alabama Infrantry Regiment, organized earlier at Richmond.

The Ninth Alabama was a fighting regiment, and Renfroe first saw action at the siege of Yorktown in April 1862. The next month Private Renfroe was with his regiment at Williamsburg, and in June he fought in the battle of Seven Pines. On June 30, he was wounded at Gaines' Mill. His wounds and assignments to detail kept him out of the fighting at Frazier's Farm, Second Manassas, and Sharpsburg in 1862, but he returned to the fighting and participated in the battle at Fredericksburg in December 1862. In 1863 the Ninth Alabama fought at Salem Church, Gettysburg, Bristow Station, and Mine Run, but Renfroe was absent on detail in every instance. The nature of his details is unknown. On January 30, 1864, Renfroe deserted.[4]

Such an inglorius end to an otherwise honorable military career may not have been the disgrace it appears on the surface. To have served on various details, fought in five battles, and been wounded in one hardly constituted a dishonorable record. His desertion may have been an act of cowardice, but his previous record makes that improbable. It is possible that as the oldest child in the family, Renfroe, like many other Confederate soldiers, went home to help out on the farm and never returned to his regiment. In any event, his military career ended in January 1864.

With the war over, Renfroe, still a young man in his twenties, faced the future and the problems of Reconstruction with more

[4] Original Roll Record of Company G, Ninth Alabama Infantry Regiment; on file at the Military Records Division, Department of Archives and History.

optimism than did many of his older comrades. He began a courtship with Mary E. Shepherd of Butler County, and won her with his virility and charm. The two were married on September 2, 1865, by Justice of the Peace Coleman O'Gwynn at the Butler County Courthouse.[5] Where Steve and "Mollie," as he called his wife, resided at first is unknown. By their second year of marriage they lived on a farm a few miles from Calhoun Station in Lowndes County, located between Montgomery and Butler counties. The Renfroes shared their house with Mollie's sister and her husband, Dr. Thomas Mills. Renfroe and Mills, a well known man who had resided at Greenville and Montgomery, worked the farm together and Mills also practiced medicine.

This dual household arrangement might have lasted indefinitely but for an improbable whimsey of fate. On July 9, 1867, Mollie and her sister began an argument over some chickens. This sisterly spat undoubtedly grew into proportions far beyond its original importance because when the men returned home, each wife reported her grievance to her husband. Tempers flaring, the husbands became involved in a really serious dispute. So intense did the quarrel become that Renfroe left the room only to return shortly with a double-barreled shotgun. Although the details of the fight are unknown, some provocation from Mills caused Renfroe to raise his weapon abruptly and fire point bank. Knocked backwards by the blast's impact, the physician fell dead.

This family squabble instigated the first flight—the first of many more to follow in Renfroe's enigmatic career as a fugitive from justice. He fled from Lowndes County rather than remain to face the consequences of this murder. The community became excited and organized a pursuit. Newspapers reported the affair but refused to condemn Renfroe.[6] Two weeks after Mills was killed, Governor Robert M. Patton issued a proclamation

[5] Butler County Marriage Licenses 1865-1868, 60; on file at the Butler County Courthouse, Greenville, Alabama.
[6] See Greenville *Advocate*, July 11, 1867; Montgomery *Mail*, July 11, 1867; Montgomery *Daily Mail*, July 13, 1867, quoting Mobile *Evening News*.

offering $200 reward for Renfroe's capture. The details of the slaying inspired the first of countless newspaper descriptions and philosophical speculations concerning Renfroe. The more materialistically inclined—those interested in claiming the reward—were content with the state's detached description: the fugitive was "thin visaged" and slender, weighing 139 pounds. He had a fair complexion, grey eyes, black hair, and wore a light mustache.[7] The mustache became his trademark.

Renfroe never returned to Butler or Lowndes County. His family, other than his wife Mollie, and his home were cut off from him for the rest of his life. Sumter County and its county seat of Livingston became his new home.[8] A resident of the county who saw him then remarked that Renfroe "was fair and delicate looking as a girl." He was dressed in "the prettiest suit of clothes I had ever seen, a home-made check, handsomely worked and bound with silk braid. He was a handsome, tidy young fellow, and his delicate features, fair face and neat attire contrasted strikingly with the tawny, coarsely dressed ex-soldiers of the dark days after the war." [9]

In this Black Belt section of Alabama Stephen S. Renfroe was to become the protagonist on a stage of violence. He came to Sumter County a stranger, and in spite of all the lives there which he touched and changed he died a stranger. The people never knew him.

---

[7] Governor's Proclamation Book December 24, 1860, to December 26, 1881, Book G; on file at the Department of Archives and History.

[8] Tallahassee *Weekly Floridian*, July 29, 1886, quoting Birmingham *Iron Age*, July 18, 1886. Unsubstantiated stories persist that members of Renfroe's family lived at least for a time in Sumter County.

[9] *Ibid.*

CHAPTER II

Sumter County and Reconstruction

I nto what kind of land did Renfroe wander to seek refuge?
Among what kind of people did he ply his gifts? The
answers to these questions are important because the area
and circumstances were to supply the backdrop for a turbulent
career spanning the next twenty years. Sumter County had a
deep history monumented by the name itself. Created in December
1832, the county was carved out of the Choctaw Indian
Nation and named for General Thomas Sumter, a South Carolina
hero of the American Revolution.

The county was a rich, verdant region, bounded on the west
by Mississippi, on the east by the wine-colored Tombigbee River
(to the north and south lay Choctaw and Pickens counties). Its
one thousand square miles of undulating black prairie lands
were interspersed with ridges and hills. Cutting across the
county were the languid Noxubee and Sucarnatchie rivers and a
number of large creeks. Near the county's center and bordering
Mississippi was the Flat Woods, a belt of post oak flatwoods
varying in width from five to eight miles and forming the perfect
refuge for a man like Renfroe.

Sumter County was settled early in the nineteenth century
by men from Virginia and the Carolinas. By the 1850's the area
was a leading producer of wheat and cotton, dotted with
medium-sized farms but dominated by large plantations worked

by hundreds of slaves. In 1860 the county's 5,919 whites, 18,091 slaves, and 25 free Negroes gave it rank among the state's top fifteen slaveholding counties. Broadcloth aristocrats maintained a benevolent despotism over the yeoman white majority and controlled, not always so benevolently, the slaves who outnumbered the total white population more than three to one.

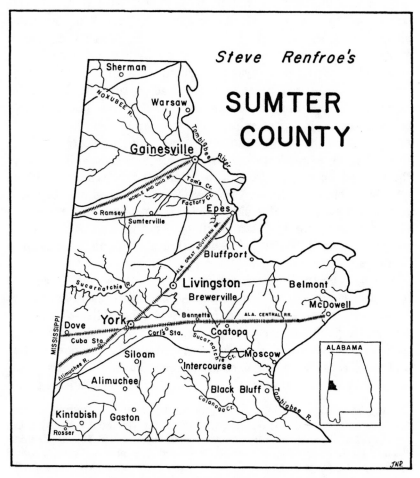

Laid out in 1833, Livingston derived its name from Edward Livingston, friend of Andrew Jackson and prominent politician. It was at Livingston, an oak-lined village of two thousand people, that the wealth and civilization of Sumter's gregarious ante-bellum society centered. Joseph G. Baldwin, author of the widely read and important *The Flush Times of Alabama and Mississippi*, was living at Livingston when his book was published in 1853. Gainesville and Gaston were other important towns, and there were numerous communities such as Warsaw, Sumterville, Ramsey's Station, Belmont, Moscow, and Cuba.[1]

Such was the country that Renfroe found. Although the postwar population was about the same as that of 1860, the scene had changed. Proud planters, now penniless, joined the yeomen as farmers. Former slaves not only were free but soon would vote and hold office. They congregated daily at the courthouse square, lounging around the bored well, a town landmark located in the square's northwest corner. The courthouse, a tall, boxlike frame building with numerous small windows, dominated a square that was ranged on two sides by stores and offices. The freedmen's broad drawls contrasted strikingly with the clipped speech of Federal soldiers and Northern civilians who had come South. At Choctaw House, opened in 1836 and badly in need of repairs since 1861, the register had never reflected such a cosmopolitan clientele. Another inn, Bell's Hotel, would be opened in 1872. A British traveler found Livingston a "considerable town . . . ." [2]

The newcomers, or carpetbaggers, rapidly became objects of hate, accused by the native citizens—sometimes truly, sometimes falsely—of manipulating the Negroes at the polls in order to put the Republican party in power. There were also the scalawags. These native Southerners cooperated with the new regime and were considered undesirable at best, traitors at worst. Dislike for the scalawags equalled or surpassed the local contempt

----

[1] *Eighth Census* (1860), 8. See also Anthony Winston Dilliard, "History of Sumter County," reprinted in 1869 in the Gainesville *News;* typed copy on file at the Sumter County Courthouse; Nelle Morris Jenkins, *Pioneer Families of Sumter County, Alabama* (Tuscaloosa, 1961), *passim;* R. D. Spratt, *History of the Town of Livingston, Alabama* (n.p., 1928), *passim;* James Benson Sellers, *Slavery in Alabama* (University, 1950), 168, 247-248, 263.

[2] Robert Somers (with an introduction by Malcolm C. McMillan), *The Southern States Since the War 1870-71* (University, 1965), 158; see also Mobile *Register,* October 21, 1874, quoting New York *Tribune.*

for the carpetbaggers. One white Sumter countian who joined
the Republican party wrote, "In the loss of property, the loss of
business, and by social proscription I am not only brought to
want but very nearly ruined." [3] His lot was an example of the
natives' wholesale condemnation and ostracism of their own
who joined the enemy's camp. The setting of Reconstruction was
not one which lent itself to rational analysis or objective evalua-
tions.

The Republican power structure in Sumter County, as elsewhere in the South, was based on the Negro vote. Carpetbaggers
and scalawags, constituting only a sprinkling of the population,
made the basic political and economic decisions. The system was
sustained by Union soldiers and such agencies as the Freedmen's Bureau, the Union League (sometimes called the Loyal
League or more simply, the League), and various educational
and religious groups.

Native Southerners, and none more than the outwardly placid,
easy-going Black Belt contingent, harbored a scathing contempt
for their "Yankee rulers." In turn, respresentatives from the
Federal government came to distrust the defeated Southerners.
As a result, passive resistance turned to hate and violence. According to a Northern reporter, "The old Union soldiers will
remember the tall, scrawny, long-haired Alabamians they used
to meet in battle, how bold they were, how enduring, and how
relentlessly cruel when chance or hard fighting gave them a
victory. These are the sort of men that inhabit Sumter County."[4]

Whether Renfroe was ever tried for the slaying of Dr. Mills
or whether the charges were dropped is not known. The acquaintance who had admired his checked suit said that Renfroe's wife

[3] Samuel A. Hale to Governor William H. Smith, July 2, 1868, Governor's Correspondence; on file at the Department of Archives and History. Reconstruction literature is immense, controversial, and growing.
See Bernard A. Weisberger, "The Dark and Bloody Ground of Reconstruction Historiography," *Journal of Southern History*, XXV (November,
1959), 427-447. Indispensable for Reconstruction in Alabama is Walter
L. Fleming, *Civil War and Reconstruction in Alabama* (New York, 1905),
but see also Sarah Van V. Woolfolk, "Carpetbaggers in Alabama: Tradition Versus Truth," *Alabama Review*, XV (April, 1926), 133-144.

[4] "Curtis," writing in Chicago *Inter Ocean*, October 9, 1874.

joined him in Sumter County in 1868. Only twenty-two, Mollie died of unknown causes on August 2, 1868, and was buried at the Bethel Cemetery in Sumter County.[5]

Renfroe was hardly a man to remain single long. By 1869 he had attracted the favorable attention of Mary M. Sledge, oldest daughter of one of the county's most prominent men. Mary fell in love with the daredevil, swashbuckling Renfroe. The couple was married by the Reverend W. H. Palsy on November 20, 1869, just three days after "Pattie," as she was better known, celebrated her twentieth birthday. Of serene nature, the young bride had attended Judson Institute at Marion in neighboring Perry County and was a strong worker in the Missionary Baptist Church.

It seems certain that Pattie, described as "ladylike, thoughtful, considerate and self-sacrificing," attempted to restrain some of Renfroe's reckless impulses. If she did not know the particulars, Pattie was aware of the general outlines of her husband's double life: during these years he was both a respectable farmer and a leading member of the Ku Klux Klan. Turning to the soil in 1870, Renfroe had purchased 355 acres of land (he paid $1,000 cash and signed notes to pay the remaining $2,000) and appeared to be accepting if not enjoying the burdens of Reconstruction. He served on county juries three times in 1871, collecting in all $18.70 for his civic duties.[6]

Pattie became suddenly ill in the summer of 1871 and died at her family home near Payneville on July 11. Renfroe interred her at the Old Side Cemetery. Some sense of sentiment caused him to move Mollie's body from Bethel and bury her by the side of Pattie.[7]

[5] No indictments exist in the Sumter or Lowndes county courthouses.

[6] Sumter County Marriage Records, 1864-1873, 304; on file at the Department of Archives and History; Livingston *Journal*, May 5, July 21, 1871; Sumter County Deeds, Book T, November 9, 1870, 545; on file at the Sumter County Courthouse; Jenkins, *Pioneer Families*, 56; authors' interview with Mrs. Elizabeth Bell Stegall, Emelle, Alabama, June, 1964. Mrs. Stegall, an authority on Sumter County, permitted the use of her files.

[7] Livingston *Journal*, July 21, 1871; tombstone inscriptions from Stegall files.

Once again without a wife, Renfroe soon was courting Cherry V. Reynolds, who lived at Livingston but had family ties at Meridian, Mississippi. (Meridian, only thirty-eight miles away and described as "sprawling over sandy mounds in a wide open bosom of the forest," was the nearest town of any size.[8] Many Sumter County residents traded there, and it was a principal supplier for Livingston wholesale merchants.) Cherry, twenty-three and renowned for her beauty, was as susceptible to the broad-shouldered stranger as the others had been. She and Renfroe were married at Meridian on January 9, 1873. This was to be his last marriage. Apparently Cherry was a person of means because sometime during 1873 she loaned Renfroe $600.

On the surface, Renfroe led a quiet and unexceptional life. In 1872 and 1873 he was paid for rendering jury service and acquired a reputation as a good farmer. On one occasion he raised a turnip that measured twenty-five inches in circumference in two directions and twenty-seven inches in two other directions. Renfroe's amazing product was celebrated in the Livingston paper. He reported the first cotton bloom in the county on June 11, 1874.[9]

Through these years Reconstruction went grimly on. After President Andrew Johnson's lenient plan of dealing with the South was overthrown and Radical Reconstruction installed, the former Confederate states fought back. Many Southerners had expected harsh treatment in 1865, but it was not until 1867 that military occupation and Radical Reconstruction began. Since the war had ended two years ago and Southerners believed themselves controlled by miscreants and persecuted without reason, they sought extra-legal means of resistance. Their dream became the restoration of home rule: in counties like Sumter with heavy concentrations of Negroes, the desire for redemption was doubly intense.

[8] Somers, *Southern States Since the War*, 150.

[9] Marriage Records December 25, 1867, to January 14, 1879, Book 1-A, 307; on file at the Lauderdale County Courthouse, Meridian, Mississippi; see also Ms. Census for Sumter County, 1870, 196. For the loan see Sumter County Deeds, Book 10, July 19, 1880, 558. See also Livingston *Journal*, February 21, August 29, September 26, December 19, 1873; June 19, 1874.

To the average Sumter countian, lost in the confusion of his shattered society and battered from all sides by alien political pressures, life was a bitter series of insults and ignominies. He yearned for someone to step into the leadership vacuum created by this storm of divisive enmity. It seemed inevitable that Renfroe—groomed by circumstances and inclination—would fill this position. The doubts that people had about him were offset by his obvious strength and courage, and in the turbulent Reconstruction years, a man's past was seldom questioned. Yet as Renfroe became more widely known, speculations naturally followed. Some suspected that he was indeed a fugitive from justice; others believed the name Renfroe to be an alias; he was, according to some reports, a deserter from the Union Army. He was known to have come from Chattanooga, from Kentucky, and from Georgia. Renfroe never saw fit to satisfy their curiosity. He did, however, provide the focus of personality and dash needed to motivate action against the Radical regime. He shared with the native citizen a deep hatred for the political and social revolution that accompanied Reconstruction, and his methods, dramatic and brutal, were quite effective.

Of all the defensive expedients none were more controversial than the formation and activities of the Ku Klux Klan. If ever a man and an organization seemed destined for each other, Steve Renfroe and the Klan fit that design. The handsome plowman who walked behind his mule by day with an erect, athletic carriage played a different role at night.

CHAPTER III

Prelude to Violence

In the spring and summer of 1865, ragged Confederates returned to Sumter County to find their familiar world vanished forever. They were confused and aimless in a situation without precedent. Planters and farmers tried to repair the damages of war and plant their crops but were retarded by rusty plows, strayed and stolen stock, sagged fences, caved in wells, and devastated lands. Bitter defeat lay behind; an uncertain future loomed ahead. State and county governments were disrupted, citizens were financially prostrate, and, most important of all, the mode and status of labor had been revolutionized. The newly freed slaves came and went as they pleased, and, aided by the Freedmen's Bureau, made work contracts. Military forces would soon appear to supervise elections and uphold the authority of the United States.

A desperate camaraderie prevailed in the first years after Appomattox. While examples of racial conflict occurred, to a surprising degree, relations between the whites and Negroes were good. Sumter County Negroes formed a benevolent association called the "Friendly Society," in which efforts were made to achieve white and Negro cooperation. When the Friendly Society met at the courthouse, pre-war slaveholders—many wearing faded uniforms carefully patched and somehow dignified—were frequently featured speakers.

John G. Harris spoke for most Sumter countians when he declared, "It should be the earnest desire of all men to see our state thoroughly reorganized and reconstructed, and her civil government set in motion." He realized, "We have been wandering in chaos and confusion ever since the close of the War; and now it behooves all to work together for the desired end, that of restoring peace and harmony among our people." [1]

Although both were destitute, the Negro's plight was far worse than that of the average white. Yet "As far as we can learn," a local paper remarked, the Negroes "have generally gone to work pretty cheerfully . . . ." [2] Nor was there any dispute when a Republican wrote, "Reconstruction in good faith, is the magnet that will draw capital, and industry to this devastated land." [3] On one occasion whites and Negroes held a joint Fourth of July barbecue and flag presentation that was attended by over two thousand people. Although the crowd gathered at Ayer's Grove near Livingston listened to orators expound different political gospel, good will and sobriety prevailed. [4]

The euphoric atmosphere ended abruptly when the first act in a series of Congressional measures providing for military occupation and the reformation of state government passed in 1867. Thus was inaugurated the bitter era of Radical Reconstruction. Scalawags became articulate, carpetbaggers arrived, and soon these men and their activities, both real and imagined, helped create the conditions that resulted in night riding orders such as the Ku Klux Klan. However well intentioned—and many so-called carpetbaggers and scalawags were sincerely dedicated to bettering the conditions of Negroes—their unwelcome intrusion provoked a spirit of unlawful retaliation. Too often the innocent as well as the guilty were made to suffer. In Reconstruction's story, the chapter written in Sumter County featured Steve Renfroe prominently in its cast of characters.

Those Northerners who worked quietly and with good results had their efforts obscured by the machinations of a few carpet-

[1] J. G. Harris to William H. Smith, July 2, 1868, Governor's Correspondence.

[2] Livingston *Journal*, January 19, 1867.

[3] Livingston *Messenger*, June 13, 1867, quoting Selma *Republican*.

[4] Livingston *Journal*, July 13, 1867.

baggers who scarcely bothered to conceal their goal of exploitation. The native whites soon reacted negatively to all carpetbaggers, opposing their acts and denouncing their programs. One disgruntled editor offered a reward for the capture or location of any carpetbagger who was not holding public office.[5] The Northerners found a scattering of local scalawags, in addition to the Negroes, who lent them support and formed an alliance. It was unfortunate and unfair that all scalawags—whether good or evil, honest or corrupt—were placed indiscriminately into a gallery of charlatans and opportunists, but such was the case.

Two native Southerners who earned the ire of their kindred were Probate Judge James A. Abrahams and Daniel Price. Judge Abrahams was appointed to his office, a six-year term following the resignation of Tobias Lane, an Ohio carpetbagger. Although Lane's first name was corrupted locally to "To-Buy-Us," he was admittedly a gentleman, a man of ability. He was elected in the controversial February 1868 elections, but considering the election invalid, he declined to serve and soon returned to his native state.[6] As Lane's successor, Abrahams had pursued a consistent ideological course in opposing secession, remaining at home during the war, and making no effort to conceal his reputation as a Union man. His sentiments earned him scorn and ostracism, but he was not molested. The tall judge was portly and handsome. He was dignified, erect, and distinguished by a well groomed and full flowing sepia-colored beard. So courtly that he was called "His Serene Highness," Abrahams was a capable and conscientious judge. Even though an opponent called him "a very estimable man," Abrahams was a constant and bitter reminder to the white people of their defeat.[7]

---

[5] *Ibid.*, January 11, 1868.

[6] *Testimony Taken by the Joint Select Committee to Inquire Into the Conditions of Affairs in the Late Insurrectionary States. Alabama. (Washington, 1872).* See Vol. III for testimony of Samuel A. Hale, 1819, 1825; Livingston *Journal*, January 18, February 15, 20, 1868.

[7] *Alabama Testimony*, III, John C. Gillespie, 1609. See additional testimony of Samuel A. Hale, 1861; Benjamin F. Herr, 1715; Herr, "Reconstruction in Sumter County," 14.

Of all the scalawags in the county, none was so hated as Daniel Price. His checkered past caught up with him in bits and pieces but was never pasted together into a whole, believable story. Apparently Price was a native of Wetumpka, Alabama, and served two years in the state penitentiary before being pardoned. He entered the Confederate army but supposedly deserted to serve with Union forces. After serving as a Freedman's Bureau official at nearby Demopolis, Price drifted into Livingston in 1868 and became the first white man in the county to teach a Negro school. To aid him in teaching he brought his mother and sister to Livingston. The ladies were respected, but Price lived openly with a Negro mistress.

He also boarded with Negroes. While the whites considered Price an unconscionable rascal and shunned him, he suffered no violence. It was not long before Price became involved with the Union League, organized at Livingston in June 1867. Price became influential with the Negroes, and, according to his critics, wielded an almost mesmeric power over them. On one occasion he issued fulminations against the whites and threatened to bring over two thousand Negroes into Livingston and destroy the town. On another he told a Negro audience, "If you are insulted by a white man, return it. If you are struck by a white man, strike him back. And if you cannot get satisfaction in the day-time, take a club or a chunk, and get it at night." [8]

Price held several offices, some elected and some appointed. He served variously as circuit clerk, registrar of voters, census taker, superintendent of education, and postmaster. Democrats knew him as "Head Centre of the League in this County." He was a perceptive, bold man who performed a valuable service in teaching the Negroes, but he was intractable and ruthless. His actions so outraged the whites that increasingly he began receiving verbal and written threats to his life. In 1870 he resigned his position as circuit clerk and moved to Meridian. There is a

---

[8] Livingston *Journal*, July 10, 1868. See also *Alabama Testimony*, III, John G. Harris, 1589-1590; John C. Gillespie, 1615-1616; Thomas Cobbs, 1623, 1640; Letters Received, May 13, 1867, Freedman's Bureau at Demopolis, Alabama, Record Group 105, National Archives, Washington, D.C.

strong implication that his departure was made certain by threats from Renfroe. At least Price's connection with Livingston and Renfroe did not end when be moved to Mississippi.[9]

The beginning of Radical Reconstruction meant a polarization of political attitudes. Before the Civil War, Sumter County had witnessed close political contests between the Whigs and Democrats, but the former adversaries coalesced into an organization called the Democratic and Conservative party (the word Conservative would be dropped later). The political marriage was one of necessity to its participants who knew of no other way to combat their Republican enemies.

Former Whigs had little choice. One resident lamented that he and an acquaintance were "almost down with the same disease—we are old-line Whigs." Another spoke of a friend: "he is an 'old line whig.' but votes with the democratic party. He is like a great many of us; we have got no party; we are lost, absorbed." [10] The divisions became bitterly drawn: the whites, by an overwhelming majority, became staunch Democrats. The Republicans were composed in the main of Negroes who were supported and directed by carpetbaggers and scalawags.

Organizing the Negro vote became the Union League's main function. After Price and others helped establish the League, its members held frequent meetings at a private residence in Livingston, then moved to a room over a store, and finally to one over a bakery. The members elected John W. Little, a Negro, president. Disfranchised natives claimed that white Republicans preached race hatred and encouraged the League to hold military drills at night.[11]

The issue of political power soon got a test. The spring or military registration of voters in 1867 saw 3,671 Negroes register and only 957 whites. Numerous whites were ineligible under

[9] Livingston *Journal*, June 22, 1867; July 31, 1868; Gainesville *News*, September 23, 1868; *Alabama Testimony*, III, Edward W. Smith, 1956-1958; Samuel A. Hale, 1816, 1818.

[10] *Alabama Testimony*, III, Allen E. Moore, 1586, and John C. Gillespie, 1607.

[11] *Ibid.*, Benjamin F. Herr, 1662-1663; Livingston *Journal*, December 14, 1867.

the Reconstruction acts, while others simply refused to participate in what they considered a debased government. In the
October 1867 election for calling a Constitutional Convention,
only twenty negative votes, presumably cast by Democrats, were
registered. Victorious Republicans cast 3,276 ballots despite
charges that Negroes were voted like cattle. After the document
known widely as the carpetbag constitution was drawn up, it
was submitted for ratification in February 1868. Elections were
held at the same time for various offices. All over Alabama
white citizens boycotted the polls; they hoped to defeat the constitution by preventing it from receiving a majority of affirma-
tive votes from registered voters. The voting in Sumter County
went on for three days amid imputations of gross voting and
registration irregularities. At the polling place in the Livingston
courthouse a Negro boy kept a huge fire going although its
warmth was felt by less than one per cent of the registered
white voters. Across the state the strategy seemed to have
worked, but the victory was short-lived as military and Congressional authorities simply decreed that the constitution would
go into effect in June 1868.[12]

Under the Union League's direction the Negroes on several
occasions armed themselves and marched along the streets of
Livingston. During the presidential campaign of 1868 they
staged a parade to promote the cause of General Grant. Some
walked through Livingston to the steady cadence of a drum
while others, carrying swords, rode plow horses forming a kind
of pseudo-cavalry. They cheered for Grant, passed through town
to a spring on the outskirts, and listened to Daniel Price make a
speech. Undoubtedly the Negroes regarded the event as a holi-
day and enjoyed themselves with uninhibited antics. A witness
confessed that the good humored procession baffled description.
"It presented," he wrote, "the usual display of colored calico,
gaudy head-dresses and indescribable uniforms. The parade was
doubtless intended to be military in character, and the manner in

---

[12] *Alabama Testimony*, III, Benjamin F. Herr, 1678; Livingston *Journal*,
September 29, October 5, 1867; January 25, February 15, 1868; D. H. Trott
to W. T. Hatchett, February 24, 1868, Freedmen's Bureau Files; on file at
the Department of Archives and History.

which the numerous officers deported themselves, running forward, running backward, running sidewise, giving all sorts of
military commands at all kinds of times, had to be seen and
heard to be apreciated." [13]

The return march through town was interrupted by a group
of Negro Democrats who gave vocal approval of their presidential candidate, Horatio Seymour. Serious difficulty was
avoided when Price persuaded the Negroes to disperse.[14]

Radical victories were inexorable, and by the summer of 1868
white and Negro Republicans, having won smashing triumphs,
were firmly in political control. Democrats made limited but
futile efforts to assert themselves. For example, Mayor Edward
W. Smith issued a proclamation against armed organizations,
·but Negroes appeared on the Livingston streets in drill formation with bugles, drums, and fifes. Officers with side arms met
them outside of town, passed out Republican tickets, and
escorted the newly enfranchised Negroes to the polls. One white
man swore he saw Democratic election tickets taken from
Negroes and stamped into the dirt. The irate accuser claimed
such acts of outright intimidation by the Union League were
frequent.[15]

In addition to the better known Radical office holders, Ben
Bardwell, an illiterate Negro, was elected solicitor; Negroes
George Houston and Ben Inge, neither of whom could write,
were elected to the state legislature. A literate Negro named
Richard Harris was elected sheriff, although he declined to ac-
cept the office.[16]

[13] Livingston *Journal*, July 31, 1868. For accounts of the Union League
see *ibid.*, April 25, July 10, 31, August 7, 1868.

[14] *Ibid.*, July 31, 1868.

[15] *Alabama Testimony*, III, Benjamin F. Herr, 1678; Livingston *Journal*,
November 6, 13, 1868.

[16] The military stationed in Livingston were not without blame. One
lieutenant made military arrests in the spring of 1868 and tried to coerce
money from those arrested. He was later cashiered from the army. See
Alabama Testimony, III, Edward Smith, 1958-1959; see also testimony of
Reuben Chapman, Jr., 1942; Benjamin F. Herr, 1662. The Negro Inge, who
had been a pious man, was supposedly corrupted at the state legislature
and died of acute alcoholism within three months. See testimony of Samuel
A. Hale, 1862. See also Livingston *Journal*, July 31, 1868.

Such was the situation that caused the whites to fight back. In the violence that occurred during these years, the Negro was least to blame. Stultified by decades of rigid class restrictions, the Negro made courageous and determined efforts to adjust to freedom. Yet the change in his status from slave to freedman was too abrupt, too revolutionary in the view of many native whites. A psychological backlash was unavoidable as defeated Southerners simply could not accept on a basis of equality the people who had been their chattel property a few years earlier.

John C. Gillespie, the oldest citizen of Livingston, explained to a Congressional committee in 1871 how a majority of the people felt:

There is a disposition on the part of southern people here not to allow negroes to be impudent to them. They don't like that. They don't like for negroes they have formerly owned to be impudent or saucy to them. No man likes to take that in this country; and if one of them should speak sharply to a negro, and the negro should speak sharply back to him again, very likely the white man would not be pleased at it. I don't know how it is generally, but I know I wouldn't like for a negro to be impudent. I cannot help it. It is part of my nature. I have been raised up with them here, and I have been in the habit of controlling what few I have about me; and they have universally been quite obedient to me; and I have had no difficulty with them at all. But if a negro was to dispute my word I wouldn't like to take it. I would not like to take it from a white man; but I would not be at all inclined to take it from a negro. That is the feeling prevalent here in this country.[17]

The venerable gentleman, like most of his neighbors, considered himself a man of good will. His was a constrained attitude compared to that of a militant minority—the Ku Klux Klan—which came to Sumter County in 1868. The nature of that nocturnal order was the subject of considerable speculation in Livingston. The *Journal*'s editor noticed "the peaceable, honest and upright citizen, has never been molested by them—while rogues,

[17] *Alabama Testimony*, III 1603.

who take advantage of unsettled times to practice villainy, and whom the law often fails to reach, find no mercy at the hands of the Ku-Klux." [18] Renfroe and his followers soon gave the people an opportunity to observe at first hand how the occult Klan operated.

[18] March 28, 1868.

CHAPTER IV

The Troubled Land

That the Ku Klux Klan and kindred bands of regulators acturally existed in Sumter County is apparent, but the extent of their organization, membership, and activities is difficult to judge. When the hooded order and other night riders turned to arson and murder, revulsion and condemnation followed, but many native Southerners did not consider themselves free to destroy the movement. No matter how offensive the Klan's acts, it would be difficult to join the Radicals in stamping out the organization. One could at least resign from the order and some did, although the vacancies were filled by younger, truculent men. Yet there were practical reasons for restraining the Klan: it became increasingly apparent that clandestine violence made the state liable to harsher retaliation by the Federal government.

The Alabama legislature under the control of the Radicals passed two acts in late 1868 to suppress "secret organizations of men disguising themselves for the purpose of committing crime and outrages." Inefficient civil servants, the chaos of the times, plus a general inability (and frequent unwillingness) of some Alabamians to enforce them, made the measures inoperative.[1] How did the people of Sumter County, the majority of whom

---

[1] Alabama *Acts* (1868), 444-446, 452-454. See William Randel, *The Ku Klux Klan: A Century of Infamy* (Philadelphia, 1965), and David M. Chal-

upheld law and order, rationalize their actions? Like other Alabamians they hoped for a speedy restoration of home rule. Then, they believed, the outrages would automatically cease or, if not, it would be up to Southerners to bring their kinsmen to justice.

Several prominent residents of the county denied that the Klan existed or insisted that its purpose was not to disturb the peace but to shield and protect society. John G. Harris, who was widely respected as a law-abiding citizen, had never seen Klansmen parading and believed that mob violence came from personal not political reasons, at least in most cases. He did not think there was a formal organization, although "there are men who band together occasionally just merely to avenge themselves for some real or supposed outrage." [2]

In 1871 Sheriff Allen E. Moore (the Negro sheriff-elect Harris was replaced by W. W. Dillard who had resigned in 1869) recounted several crimes and outrages committed in the past but knew of no bodies of men who rode at night and whipped Negroes. Turner Reavis—former Whig, judge, and state senator—contended that the Klan operated only sporadically and that its membership was confined to lawless, dissipated men. Local leaders Thomas Cobbs and Edward C. Smith did not think the Klan had ever existed in the county. Smith called the crimes "sporadic eruptions, growing out of the revolutionary times." [3]

Samuel A. Hale, a Republican, condemned the disgraceful state of affairs. He believed the trouble came from worthless county officials, most of whom were Republicans. Most people opposed lawlessness, but the Klan undoubtedly existed. According to Hale, it was founded in Sumter County by a man from Mississippi. "I do not hear of anybody being brought to justice

---

mers, *Hooded Americanism: The First Century of the Ku Klux Klan* . . . (Garden City, 1965) for recent works; Stanley F. Horn, *Invisible Empire* (Boston, 1939) is still of value. For Alabama see James Leroy Taylor, "History of the Ku Klux Klan in Alabama 1865-1874," Unpublished master's thesis, Auburn University, 1957.

2 For Harris' statement see *Alabama Testimony*, III, 1599.

3 *Ibid.*, 1976, for Smith; 1578, for Moore, 1636, for Cobbs; I, 331-333, for Reavis.

here," Hale thundered. "Our courts of law are a farce and a sham." The self-appointed regulators could not be stopped. Officers of the law would not resist the marauders because they "are afraid of them. They are afraid to do anything—they are paralyzed by them." [4]

One man declared that the Klan consisted of bands of two or three dozen men and operated during the late hours of night. Denying the presence of a formal order, another citizen contended there was a "mere combination" who dealt with obnoxious men but admitted there might be retribution if a Klansman informed on one of his fellow members. He and other men pointed out that when a group of men decided to engage in depredations it was difficult or impossible to stop them. [5]

It seems likely that the Klan did not exist to the extent of having formal rules and prescribed regalia. Nor were there many elaborate signs and countersigns or ostentatious trappings of mystery. Undoubtedly there were outlaws and ruffians who posed as Klansmen and used the order as a front for private crimes. Whatever their misdeeds, the Klan would get the blame. Yet there were men who were members of the Ku Klux Klan, and in view of testimony from many sources, they were led by Renfroe.

The order was largely local, although the members operated in adjoining counties and in Mississippi. Klan sorties were both personal and political, directed in the main against Negroes and Radicals. This form of justice was deplored once threats turned into whippings and lashings into murders, but at first the Klan was an expression of resistance not condemned by the white majority, embittered by what they considered the excesses of Reconstruction.

Tracing some of the era's more spectacular events reveals the manner in which the Klan and various lawless groups operated, yields insight into the temper of the times, and shows Renfroe in action.

---

[4] *Ibid.*, III, 1822, 1820.
[5] *Ibid.*, Reuben A. Meredith, 1771-1772; see also testimony of John C. Gillespie, 1606, 1610, 1613; and Benjamin F. Herr, 1685, 1703.

In August 1868 a white Mississippian killed a Negro near Livingston without reason and in cold blood. The murderer was held in the Livingston jail for over a year, but was finally freed when an armed mob of some sixty men overpowered the jailor and released him. He was never recaptured. Speaking for the people of Sumter County, one editor called "upon the Legislature to devise some means to *protect the County Jail!* or abolish it althogether." [6] Asked to speculate about where the escapee might have fled, Sheriff Moore replied, "God knows. I never heard of him since. The general supposition is that they let him loose." He added, "I think he is in Texas or somewhere else, God Almighty knows where." [7]

In 1868 a Negro, who apparently confessed to participating in the murder of a white man, was removed from the Livingston jail by a mob of fifteen or twenty men, taken out on the Demopolis road, shot twice, and hanged. Two or three citizens were arrested and taken to Selma for examination by military authorities, but because there was no evidence they were released.[8] Editor Herr proclaimed in his paper: "Lynch law is no remedy for such evils." When individuals took the law into their hands, "anarchy has come and there is no security for any." [9]

Another Negro, accused of killing a white man in 1871, never faced a jury. The pattern was the familiar one of a midnight raid: the jailors were disarmed and the prisoner taken by force. The body was found the next morning by Sheriff Moore and his posse. According to Moore, "He was shot worse than any piece of flesh I ever saw. He was shot, really, from the top of his head plumb to the soles of his feet." [10] The murder outraged the com-

---

[6] Gainesville *News*, February 12, 1870. See also George Houston to William H. Smith, August 17, 1868, Governor's Correspondence; *Alabama Testimony*, III, Thomas Cobbs, 1621.

[7] *Alabama Testimony*, III, 1576; see also A. E. Moore to William H. Smith, February 9, 1870, Governor's Correspondence.

[8] *Alabama Testimony*, III, Allen E. Moore, 1578; John G. Harris, 1596, 1604; Thomas Cobbs, 1621; Reuben Chapman, Jr., 1944; Edward Clement Sanders, 1799-1801, a white man whose thinking was not typical of the majority, believed the killing was an act of justice and stated that he wanted a return to slavery.

[9] Livingston *Journal*, May 2, 1868.

[10] *Alabama Testimony*, III, 1576.

munity and was denounced in the papers. How had it occurred? Why had pursuit not been organized earlier? Moore told a Congressional committee that getting men to pursue a group of desperate ruffians at night was impossible. It was not a case of cowardice so much as one of common sense. He explained, "You don't know anything about these southern people, Senator. I was born and raised with them. I am a southern man." How did Southerners differ from other people? "You stay here long enough, and you'll find out, I'll tell you." [11]

Sumter County experienced crimes that were personal and outrages, such as whippings and mutilations, that stopped short of murder. The expression being "Ku-Kluxed" was applied to any kind of mob action, and there were several examples of Negroes Ku-Kluxing whites and other Negroes. Although the hooded order carved an infamous record, on more than one occasion the white Klan whipped and drove from the county other white men for mistreating Negroes. As in every community, Northern and Southern, there were also isolated examples of savage, unreasoning murder that had no connection with politics.

There is no way to connect Renfroe with any of the cases other than those in which he was specifically named. That he participated in others—joining with men of similar views to keep the spirit of terror alive—seems highly probable. At any event, Renfroe's natural flamboyance could not be hidden for long by a white mask. Private assertions that he led the opposition to the Radicals became increasingly public. He gained wide notice because of his concern with the strange Dr. Gerard Choctteau and, less directly, an influential Negro named George Houston.

According to several accounts Dr. Choctteau, who was of French origin and spoke broken English, migrated to Alabama from Louisiana around 1853. Some said that he had killed a man at New Orleans. In 1858 Choctteau and his family moved from

---

[11] *Ibid.,* 1572-1573; see also Livingston *Journal,* November 17, 1871; and Allen E. Moore to D. L. Dalton, June 25, 1870, Governor William H. Smith's Correspondence.

Perry County and settled on a 320 acre plantation between Ramsey's Station and Sumterville, some fifteen miles north of Livingston. Choctteau enjoyed a good reputation with the people in the neighborhood and was favorably known as a competent physician. Shortly after the Civil War ended he supposedly made a startling proposition to his partner, Dr. William H. Sledge (and possibly to others), for solving the race problem. If several witnesses can be believed, Choctteau's solution to the difficulties resulting from emancipation was to poison the wells of all the Negroes in Sumter County. His mass murder plan was rejected, and shortly after this Choctteau made a complete philosophical and political switch. He rejected his former friends and courted favor with Negroes and the Radicals.[12]

An old-time resident of Livingston said of the physician that "He was a terrible noisy, blustering sort of man, and did not please anybody much." [13] The whites soon ostracized Choctteau, forcing him to trade with Negroes. Whether true or not, he was believed to be encouraging Negroes to defend their rights by engaging in acts of violence. Choctteau supposedly joined the Loyal League (which held meetings at his place) and a group of armed Negroes protected him. There were rumors of his arresting white citizens who attempted to pass by his plantation. Few, including Choctteau, would have denied that by 1868 the bizarre doctor was a Radical and "kicking up the devil all over the country." [14]

Although Choctteau had no effective political influence, he became a prime target for abuse. "I am persecuted to my life put dayly in jeopardy," he wrote in unique syntax to the governor, adding "I cannot leave my residence." "Can then a loyal man get no protection," he wondered. Choctteau claimed that in October

---

[12] *Alabama Testimony*, III, Allen E. Moore, 1574-1575, 1579, 1583-1584; John C. Gillespie, 1608; Samuel A. Hale, 1816; letter of Choctteau to Montgomery *Alabama State Journal*, December 17, 1868.

[13] *Alabama Testimony*, III, John C. Gillespie, 1608.

[14] *Ibid.*, Allen E. Moore, 1585; see also John G. Harris, 1594; John C. Gillespie, 1603; and Thomas Cobbs, 1622; Livingston *Journal*, August 28, 1868.

before the election of 1868 an armed mob came to his plantation and killed a Negro, and that on several occasions he had been fired at.[15]

The Negro who was shot was "Yankee Ben," president of the Sumterville Loyal League and a veteran of the Civil War. Apparently the armed mob was a sheriff's posse attempting to arrest one Enoch Townsend, a Negro accused of stabbing a white planter named Bryant Richardson. Townsend was known to frequent Choctteau's plantation, and the arresting parties reached the premises at night. Systematically searching the Negro cabins, they saw a figure scramble down a chimney and run across a field. When the man refused to halt, the posse opened fire believing he was Townsend. The man was killed, but upon examination the corpse turned out to be "Yankee Ben." Townsend was later caught. A frightened but determined Sumter County Negro telegraphed the governor, "Killing freedmen has become so common in Sumter there is no security send us protection or we will fight." Other Negroes were angry about the death of the Loyal League leader, and a few days later over a hundred of them, supposedly at the urging of Daniel Price, gathered arms and met at Choctteau's. This alarmed the whites, who also armed and marched on the Negroes. A clash was averted when the Negroes dispersed. Choctteau even agreed to settle his affairs and leave the country, but he was told that this was not necessary.[16]

After the elections of 1868 firmly ensconced the Radicals in power, the reaction among the whites was more bitter than ever. Choctteau said that he attempted to let matters quiet down, but

[15] Choctteau to William H. Smith, November 14, 1868, Governor's Correspondence; Choctteau to Montgomery *Alabama State Journal*, December 17, 1868.

[16] Adam Kenard to William H. Smith, October 9, 1868 (telegram); Livingston *Journal*, October 9, 1868; *Alabama Testimony*, III, Benjamin F. Herr, 1670-1671. Governor Smith's correspondence contains several letters from Freedmen's Bureau agent John L. Stelzig to his superior describing the events connected with the death of Yankee Ben. See letters of October 2, 6, 7[?], 8, 1868; see also Letters Sent and Orders Received, August-December 1868, Freedmen's Bureau at Livingston, Alabama, RG 105, National Archives.

that his house was fired into and every indignity heaped upon him. He charged that Renfroe was the leader of the mobs that oppressed him.

On Monday night December 7, 1868, Choctteau's house was fired upon while he was out gathering wood. He had a sick child, and, because of the relentless harrassment, finally decided to move to Livingston, where protection was greater. On December 8, he moved his wife and two of his children to the county seat, leaving behind an eight-year-old son and his mother-in-law. Choctteau charged that the next evening, December 9, Renfroe and the Klan appeared at his property, forced the two occupants from the house, and burned it to the ground.

"He is here a refugee, without money or anything to eat," Daniel Price, who took the doctor in, wrote a Freedmen's Bureau authority. Price demanded, "What are we to do! Can't we get soldiers to quiet this country? I hope you will send us a few if in your power." To another official, Price declared, "'The Ku Klux are still at work in this county." [17]

Choctteau argued that the loss of his house, its contents, and several cotton bales stored there had reduced him to the status of beggar. There was some dispute about the extent of Choctteau's monetary loss, and it was even suggested that the house was burned deliberately to embarrass the Klan, but to most people it seemed a clear case of arson. As a result of charges brought by Choctteau and members of his family, Renfroe and Alexander Richardson, a resident of the county, were indicted for arson. The case was still pending three years later, but the men were never tried.[18]

At Livingston, Choctteau and his family were subject to continued outrages. His home was shot into on at least one occasion, and once again the doctor named Renfroe as the author of his

[17] Daniel Price to R. A. Wilson, December 11, 1868, Governor William H. Smith's Correspondence; see also John L. Stelzig to R. A. Wilson, December 10, 1868, *ibid.;* Daniel Price to Major C. W. Pierce, Freedmen's Bureau at Demopolis, June 12, 1868, RG 105, National Archives.

[18] Choctteau to Montgomery *Alabama State Journal*, December 17, 1868; *Alabama Testimony*, III, Benjamin F. Herr, 1669; Reuben Chapman, Jr., 1940, 1953; John G. Harris, 1594; Livingston *Journal*, October 16, December 18, 1868.

troubles. Choctteau complained that Renfroe and Richardson, despite the indictments, were "at large yet and even came into town to tease and vaunt [*sic*] my feelings telling me they would [burn me out] again." By the summer of 1869 Choctteau had hired an elderly German named John Coblentz to guard his family. At one o'clock on the morning of August 13, Choctteau was awakened by the noise of his front yard fence being broken down. A party of six or eight masked men disguised in light colored clothing disfigured with paint approached the house.

The cottage had only two rooms with an open passage between them. Choctteau was alone in one room with Coblentz stationed in the other guarding the rest of the family. The phantom-like visitors broke into Coblentz's room—one of them struck a match and was peering into the gloom when the German aimed his double-barreled shotgun and fired. The buckshot's impact knocked the intruder backwards killing him instantly (his mask was found the next morning). His place was taken by a companion who, thinking Choctteau was in the room, opened fire and hit Coblentz. The German died before daybreak. No harm was done to Mrs. Jane Morris (Choctteau's mother-in-law), his wife Nancy, himself or the three children. The assailants rode away carrying the body of their companion with them.

The next morning the sheriff organized a posse, and, guided by traces of blood for several miles, went through Brewersville to Moscow. There a Negro ferryman on the Tombigbee said half a dozen men had crossed over into Marengo County at six that morning. The men who murdered Coblentz were never discovered.[19]

At the same time that the attack on Choctteau's house occurred, some members of the band opened fire on the residence of George Houston, a Negro politician who lived nearby. Houston probably had more influence with his fellow Negroes than any

[19] Choctteau to William H. Smith, May 17, 1869, Governor's Correspondence; see also E. W. Smith to *ibid.*, July 3, 1869; and James A. Abrahams to *ibid.*, July 3, 1869. See Sumter County Coroner's report quoted in *Alabama Testimony*, III, 1673-1674; and Samuel A. Hale, 1817, 1820-1821; John G. Harris, 1594-1595; John C. Gillespie, 1603-1604; Thomas Cobbs, 1622, 1631-1632; Gainesville *News*, August 19, 1869.

other man. He had been a tailor in Livingston and was well liked
by most of the whites. His reputation was that of a kind-hearted
but bad tempered man. From the viewpoint of the whites Houston transgressed by becoming a Radical and by winning appointment as an officer of registration. Later, he was elected to
the state legislature. On various occasions he made what were
regarded as incendiary speeches to the Negroes. Once he threatened to have Livingston burned to ashes. As a dynamic leader
and confidant of Tobias Lane and various Radicals, he became a
natural target for assault.

When his home was attached, Houston returned the fire.
While the fusillade raged, his son leaped out a window and fled.
The raiders thought that Houston had escaped and ceased firing.
In reality he was still in his house and had suffered a wound
in his thigh. Houston claimed to have scored a hit himself. He
informed the governor there was no local protection "as the
most of the whites are concerned in the Klan or sit still and
wink at their doings." Demanding protection, Houston concluded, "If you can't send soldiers here *permanently* and a good
strong force, for Gods sake don't say anything about it at all,
for loud sounding proclamation[s] to the Sheriff, isn't worth
the paper on which you write them." No soldiers were sent, and
as soon as he recovered sufficiently to travel, Houston left Livingston and moved to Montgomery.[20]

The murder of Coblentz was the final act that drove Dr.
Choctteau and his family from Sumter County. He allegedly
went to Washington and got a job with the post office department only to lose it under dubious circumstances. Sheriff Moore
candidly admitted in 1871 that Choctteau had been the object of
Klan persecution and left "because he was afraid of his scalp,
I reckon." Why had the Klan tried to kill Choctteau? "Some
political matter; God only knows what. I can't tell you what." [21]

[20] George W. Houston [letter actually written by Daniel Price] to William H. Smith, August 13, 1869, Governor's Correspondence; *Alabama
Testimony,* III, Allen E. Moore, 1574-1575; John G. Harris, 1595; Benjamin
F. Herr, 1663, 1665, 1674; Reuben Chapman, Jr., 1949; John C. Gillespie,
1607-1608; Thomas Cobbs, 1622-1623; Edward W. Smith, 1956.

[21] *Alabama Testimony,* III, 1575, 1585; see also Gainesville *News,* January 22, 1870.

Choctteau was possibly a mentally disturbed man. Edward W. Smith, mayor of Livingston who had attended Princeton, said Choctteau was "about a half-cracked man." He thought most whites were members of the Klan and "he was a man whose mind seemed almost unbalanced." [22] Yet the attacks on him and Houston were obviously politically inspired. In 1874 Choctteau wrote a letter from Illinois, where he claimed to have taken refuge, accusing Renfroe of attempting to kill him. Renfroe, he charged, had killed Yankee Ben, Coblentz, and two Negroes in broad daylight near Livingston. Choctteau's sensational letter contained several distortions of fact, time, and place, but he was emphatic in denouncing "the notorious Steven Renfroe, Captain of the Ku Klux band of Sumter County, Alabama. . . ." [23]

Sheriff W. W. Dillard, unable to cope with the situation, found the murder of Coblentz a final event. "I dislike so much to be Sheriff, when such deed[s] occur so often," he wrote Governor Smith, "that I now feel it to [be] my duty to resign, and you will please accept my resignation as Sheriff of Sumter." [24] He was replaced by Allen E. Moore.

In the spring and summer of 1869—during the period of Choctteau's harrassment—Renfroe became involved, or was accused of being involved, in two senseless murders. On Saturday evening May 29, three Negroes—Caesar Davis, Frank Sledge, and Enoch Sledge—left Livingston to return home after a day of socializing and trading. They were approaching Horn's Bridge on the outskirts of town when three white men hailed them. Renfroe, Alexander Richardson (who was also indicted for burning Choctteau's home), and Robert Clay halted the Negroes in a friendly manner. All of the men were cordial and were acquaintances of long standing. For reasons never explained, one or all of the white men suddenly began shooting. Caesar Davis and Frank Sledge fell dead. Enoch Sledge, although seriously wounded, later recovered.

[22] *Alabama Testimony*, III, 1966.

[23] Choctteau's letter quoted in Montgomery *Alabama State Journal*, October 14, 1874.

[24] W. W. Dillard to William H. Smith, August 14, 1869, Governor's Correspondence.

Citizens of Sumter, acquainted with violence but not inured to it, were angered and bewildered. Mayor Edward W. Smith of Livingston denounced the wanton murders and demanded justice. He declared, "there is no question of partisan warfare, or party expediency, but it is the great and momentous question involving the life, safety, & civil liberty of the citizens."[25] County Solicitor Reuben Chapman, Jr. believed them "the most malignant murders ever committed in this state," and asserted, "It is time an example should be made of some of these desperadoes."[26]

Other residents were equally concerned. The governor was told "the freedmen behaved quite creditably under the circumstances of this atrocious murder and . . . nine tenths of the whites openly condemn it."[27] Several prominent citizens argued that offering rewards for the men would only warn them. They had already fled to the Flat Woods or into Lauderdale and Kemper counties in Mississippi; it seemed probable that the best strategy would be to employ a detective. He could come to the county, quietly stalk the men, and apprehend them. I. F. Hammond, an investigator who came from Montgomery, made optimistic reports in June and July. He was confident the men were working with the Klan and that he could find them.

Strangely, no arrests were ever made. After Renfroe and the others returned to Sumter County in a few weeks, no more was heard from Hammond. There was little evidence and an understandable lack of witnesses. On the basis of extant material, Renfroe, by common opinion, participated in the crimes, though there is no actual proof of his guilt. The shootings defy explanation, although Detective Hammond advanced one: "political cause is the only cause that can be assigned for this mysterious affair."[28]

[25] E. W. Smith to William H. Smith, June 4, 1869, *ibid.* See also Gainesville *News*, June 3, 1869.

[26] Reuben Chapman Jr., to William H. Smith, June 6, 1869, Governor's Correspondence.

[27] A. W. Dillard to William H. Smith, June 5, 1868, *ibid.*

[28] I. F. Hammond to Col. D. L. Dalton and Major C. H. Scott, June 26, 1869, *ibid.*

In the summer of 1870 Circuit Judge Luther N. Smith, a native of Massachusetts who was unpopular in his own right, received a letter from Daniel Price resigning his position as clerk of the Circuit Court. Price frankly stated that if he remained at Livingston he would be killed. Renfroe had helped him reach his decision. Not long afterward Price was prominently mentioned not only as a leading teacher of the freedmen in Meridian but as a strong possibility for mayor. Price's quick rise to prominence in Mississippi was aided by his persuading Sumter County Negroes to move to Meridian. Because of the acute labor shortage any loss of workers was resented, and, when it was learned that the hated Price was the instigator, action seemed indicated.

One of Sheriff Moore's deputies was a Negro named Adam Kennard. Moore shrewdly used Kennard to serve various legal papers on Negroes and, when necessary, to make arrests. The deputy proved himself an able lawman.[29] But when Moore sent Kennard to Meridian to arrest several Negroes accused of breaking work contracts and various crimes, Meridian officials were dubious about the Negro's lack of credentials. Kennard's venture was not successful. On a return visit to Meridian, Kennard was taken from his boarding house at night and Ku-Kluxed. Kennard claimed that Price and a group of Negroes robbed him, took him into the woods, stripped him, and administered a severe beating. Kennard had Price arrested as having violated a state law against the Ku Klux Klan; the trial was set for February 1871.

Renfroe gathered a group of men, varying according to several estimates from 40 to 150 men, to accompany Kennard to Meridian to see justice done. Renfroe's men rode into town, supposedly stacked arms in the street, and registered at the Phoenix Hotel (one allegation had the men refusing to pay their bills). The possibility of trouble was so imminent that the mayor postponed Price's trial. The disappointed Alabamians returned to Livingston but took with them several Sumter County Negroes whom they had spotted at the Meridian depot.

[29] *Alabama Testimony*, III, Allen E. Moore, 1587; John C. Gillespie, 1607.

The Negroes had supposedly fled robbery charges in Alabama. Their abduction infuriated Meridian's Negro community, and a party of unknown men fired on the train during the return trip.

Feeling ran so high that Price's trial was postponed a second time and reset for early March. After a conference, town leaders decided that the best policy would be to release Price without trial and order him to leave town. This was done, but unplacated Radical leaders and Negroes decided to protest against the previous kidnappings and Price's forced exodus from town. On Saturday, March 4, they held an indignation meeting. Among the several speeches were some so incendiary that three Negroes were arrested. They were to be tried the following morning.

News of these events reached Renfroe and other men in Sumter County (they were invariably referred to by Mississippians as the Alabama Ku Klux Klan). By horseback and by train Sumter countians began arriving at Meridian on Sunday. Joining them were men from other Alabama counties led by Joe Reynolds, a clerk in Pollard's store at Eutaw in Greene County. Reynolds was a young Georgian who had already earned a reputation as a trouble maker and ruffian. Various witnesses said that Reynolds worked closely with Renfroe. One Negro said of Reynolds, "I know him well; I know that he is a mighty man for killing niggers when he got a chance; I have seen him shoot three." [30]

---

[30] Testimony of William Horne, *Mississippi Legislative Investigation*, 52. For other testimony taken in this investigation see Sheriff Robert J. Mosely, 25; Henry Matson, 29; District Attorney J. P. Walker, 31; Harris Richardson (Negro), 51; and L. D. Belk, 33. See also *Testimony Taken by the Joint Select Committee to Inquire Into the Condition of Affairs in the Late Insurrectionary States. Mississippi* (Washington, 1872). See Vol. I for statements of O. C. French, 10, 14, 17-18. This volume contains the complete testimony of the state investigation as well. See also *Alabama Testimony*, III, Allen E. Moore, 1587; John C. Gillespie, 1607; Livingston *Journal*, February 10, March 3, 10, 1871; Jackson [Mississippi] Weekly *Clarion*, March 9, 16, 1871; Eyre Damer, *When the Ku Klux Rode in Mississippi* (New York, 1910), 349-351; Katharine Louise McGehee. "The Meridian Race Riot of 1871," unpublished honors thesis, Florida State University, 1966; George K. Shank, Jr., "Meridian: A Mississippi City at Birth, During the Civil War, and in Reconstruction," *Journal of Mississippi History*, XXVI (November, 1964), 275-282.

Conditions in Meridian, slowly rebuilding from its virtual destruction by Sherman in 1864, were already at a breaking point between the local whites and the Radicals. All that was needed was the presence of Renfroe and the Alabamians and a proper incident. This came on March 6 in the courthouse when the trial of the arrested Negroes began. A riot started in the courtroom, overflowed into the streets, spread panic through the town, and did not end until six men met their deaths either by murder or lynching.

The Meridian riot was investigated by a state legislative committee and also by a Congressional committee. In the aftermath Price fled Meridian never to be heard of again; Joe Reynolds, having left his indelible mark, hurriedly went West only a few steps ahead of various indictments pending against him. Casual as always, Renfroe went back to Livingston.

It is impossible to measure how active Renfroe was in the Meridian riot. William Sturges, Radical mayor of Meridian who had been forced to leave the city after the disturbance, wrote a lengthly letter to the New York *Tribune*. Sturges attributed part of the trouble to the Alabamians, "under the command, as I am informed, of one Renfru, who, as I believe, was with his gang. . . ." [31]

In Livingston it was common knowledge and freely discussed that Renfroe and several other men had been at Meridian during the riot. There were no public condemnations of Renfroe. John G. Harris of Livingston did not hestitate to castigate Reynolds as a worthless and vicious desperado. What of his partner, Renfroe? He was, Harris said, a man of "character . . . , a genteel man." Moreover, Renfroe was "regarded as a good citizen, and as a gentleman among the people." [32] Harris, like many other people acquainted with Renfroe, liked him. He was held in awe, viewed with respect, secretly admired. In a time when heroes were few, Renfroe—although flawed and incorrigible—was a hero.

[31] Sturges' letter quoted in Livingston *Journal*, March 24, 1871; see also New York *Daily Tribune*, March 16, 1871. The Jackson *Weekly Clarion*, March 29, 1871, quoted a letter from Theodore Sturges, brother of William, repudiating the statement of the deposed mayor.

[32] *Alabama Testimony*, III, 1601.

CHAPTER V

A Surfeit of Politics

The results of Renfroe's activities and those of other men were soon evident. By 1870 there were not more than twenty acknowledged white Republicans in Sumter County. The Klan, social pressure, economic and physical intimidation, disillusionment—all were factors in depleting the Radical ranks. Sheriff Moore did not believe Sumter County Radicals were scarce as hens' teeth, but, asked to estimate their number, replied, "Mighty few." [1]

Samuel A. Hale was convinced that had the Radicals treated loyal Republicans right there would have been 500 white party members in the county. By the summer of 1868 Negroes began withdrawing from the Union League. President John W. Little and Sydenham Porter published cards in the local paper announcing their resignations and advising their fellow Negroes to renounce the Radicals and abstain from politics.[2]

The test in Alabama and the county came in the campaign of 1870 when various offices including that of governor were to be filled. Sumter had approximately 4,000 voters, a majority of them Negroes. When the votes were totalled the surprising results revealed that the county and state had gone Democratic

---

[1] *Alabama Testimony*, III 1585-1586; John C. Gillespie, 1609, knew of only four native whites who voted for Grant in 1868; Thomas Cobbs, 1647, estimated there were only half a dozen white Republicans in the county.

[2] *Ibid.*, 1861; Benjamin F. Herr, 1665; Livingston *Journal*, August, 14, 1868.

with a Democrat elected governor. How could Sumter County which had voted so strongly for Grant in 1868 have suddenly reversed itself? There were two explanations, both partisan and both partly correct.

Democrats agreed politics had been spirited but insisted the election had been quiet, peaceable, and void of intimidation, threats, or coercion. They said the Negroes were disillusioned by the bad character of various Republicans. The Negroes were so disappointed with Radical failures that several freedmen had campaigned openly for the Democrats. The Democrats won, explained one Livingston citizen, because blacks abandoned the Union League, because the carpetbaggers had gone, and because the Democrats campaigned vigorously against Republican candidates who did not even canvass the county. The presence of federal troops at the polling places, the Democratic partisan pointed out, prevented coercion.[3] He was correct in emphasizing that intimidation did not take place at the polls because Republican requests for troops had been answered. Blue clad soldiers— Company F of the Sixteenth Infrantry whose thirty-six men were commanded by Captain William Wodemeyer—maintained order at the various ballot boxes.[4]

Republicans assigned different causes for their defeat. John Childers, an illiterate Negro, claimed he and other blacks had been whipped for political reasons. At times their oppressors wore masks but just as often did not bother with disguises. Childers believed he was persecuted because he voted the Radical ticket. Were the whippings frequent? "Yes sir; just as common as daylight." During the 1870 campaign Childers, informed a coffin was waiting for him in the event he voted Republican, voted Democratic. Were other Negroes threatened? "It was just as common as drinking is for such things as that to be." If left

[3] *Alabama Testimony*, III Benjamin F. Herr, 1679-1681; see *ibid.*, for John G. Harris, 1588, 1592; Allen E. Moore, 1586; Thomas Cobbs, 1625; Edward W. Smith, 1959-1960; Reuben Chapman, Jr., 1941.

[4] Charles Hays to William H. Smith, August 13, 1870, Governor's Correspondence. Sent from Nashville, Tennessee, for duty at the polls was an infantry company of thirty-six enlisted men and one officer. See Returns From U.S. Military Posts 1800-1916, Roll 638, Livingston, Alabama, October 1874-November 1876. These returns are on file at the National Archives.

alone how many Negroes would vote Democratic? "Not one, sir. Not a single one." [5]

Granville Bennett, a Negro, claimed it was dangerous for Negroes to vote the Radical ticket and that they were intimidated into voting Democratic. Another observer testified that Democrats used economic coercion to influence the Negro vote. Because there were few or no Republican votes cast at York, Warsaw, or Cuba in 1870, he could only conclude the Negroes had been "deterred" somehow.[6]

A leading Democrat admitted it would have been dangerous for a Republican candidate to speak at Livingston. In agreement was Reuben A. Meredith, a Gainesville resident and unsuccessful Republican candidate for the state legislature. He repeated claims that Negroes were intimidated, adding that Republicans did not canvass the county because they were afraid. Meredith said he did not leave the Gainesville area because "If I had gone to making Republican speeches around here I would have been slaughtered." [7]

The charges and counter-charges ranged back and forth: Democrats claimed legal victory and Radicals charged fraud. When the excitement had subsided, it seemed clear that the campaign of 1870 had produced some significant events.

One centered on Radical attempts to hold a nominating convention at Livingston on August 12-13. Rumors spread across Livingston and the county that Republican Congressman Charles Hays (destined to have a curious relationship with Renfroe) planned to bring two hundred armed Negroes to the convention. Hays, a legislator of considerable ability, later denied having asked Negroes to bring guns and did not come himself because of illness in his family. But the possibility of a mob sacking Livingston caused panic. A call for aid was sent out.[8] White men from the surrounding area, reinforced by men from Eutaw and Meridian, converged on Livingston. The

[5] *Alabama Testimony*, III, 1720-1726.

[6] *Ibid.*, 1738-1742, for Bennett; Samuel A. Hale, 1822, 1829.

[7] *Ibid.*, John C. Gillespie, 1617-1619; Meredith, 1784, 1775, 1779.

[8] *Ibid.*, Charles Hays, 1835-1836; Benjamin F. Herr, 1682; Gainesville *News*, August 13, 1870; for a sketch of Hays see Tuscaloosa *Blade*, October 29, 1874.

Negroes came to within two miles of town but no further, and the nominating convention was never held. Democrats were relieved and Republicans frustrated.[9]

State Republicans attempted to strengthen their chances by dispatching party luminaries on speaking forays. Several of these dignitaries appeared in West Alabama, namely Willard Warner, then a United States Senator, and Lewis E. Parsons, former Provisional Governor. They were announced as speakers at the Livingston courthouse. Later Renfroe and his followers were accused of conspiring to prevent the Republicans from speaking. Their plot, if plot there was, looked to the assassination of all three speakers, but was thwarted by a high wind that forced the politicians to move to an unscheduled speaking site on another side of the courthouse.[10]

At best the touring orators were not well received. While speaking to the large audience of Negroes and whites, they were interrupted several times by sarcastic remarks. Several young men were supposed to have flourished guns during the speaking, while one stood at the front of the audience picking his teeth with a gleaming bowie knife. Senator Warner recalled that after the speeches a group of young drunks followed the itinerant politicians to their hotel. While no harm came to the dignitaries, they had several anxious moments.[11]

Radical ineptness and Democratic determination combined to account partly for the Democratic triumph in Alabama and Sumter County. Granted, the Radicals did not campaign effectively. Also broken promises and hypocritical advisors disillusioned the Negroes. An unknown measure of intimidation, however, played its part in the victory. For on the basis of registered voters alone, it would have been difficult for the Democrats to have carried Sumter County without the night-riding exploits of Renfroe and others.

[9] *Alabama Testimony,* III, Benjamin F. Herr, 1862; Reuben A. Meredith, 1773; Gainesville *News,* August 20, 1870, quoting Livingston *Journal.*

[10] Chicago *Inter Ocean,* October 12, 1874; *Alabama Testimony,* III, John C. Gillespie, 1617-1619. That such a plan actually existed seems highly unlikely.

[11] *Alabama Testimony,* I, Willard Warner, 26; Benjamin F. Herr, III, 1711; Thomas Cobbs, 1642.

Robert B. Lindsay won the governor's race from Smith by a vote of 76,977 to 75,568, a margin of only 1,409 votes. Lindsay carried Sumter County by 617 votes. Former Governor Parsons contended, with some accuracy, that violence in Greene, Sumter, and Marengo counties had cost the Republicans the state. Yet one scholar has maintained that fratricidal struggles for state leadership in the Republican party were more responsible for the Radicals' defeat than ballot box machinations.[12]

With a national election coming up in 1872, the Republicans in Congress moved to direct action. In 1870 and 1871 the Enforcement Acts, notably the Ku Klux Klan Act of April 20, 1871, were passed. Also created was an investigating body with the cumbersome title of the Joint Select Committee on the Condition of Affairs in the Late Insurrectionary States. On the surface the committee was an objective fact-finding body, but its Republican majority was intent upon exposing Ku Klux outrages and its Democratic minority was equally determined to uncover evidence of Republican misrule. Gathering data in both Washington and throughout the South, the committee listened to a parade of witnesses who poured forth fascinating revelations. When the committee took testimony at the Livingston Courthouse from October 30 to November 3, 1871, Renfroe's name did not go unmentioned.

The Klan had lost favor when it became apparent that its activities and their attendant notoriety justified Radical Reconstruction measures. The members disbanded, and by the fall of 1871 the Klan ceased to exist in the state and in Sumter County.[13]

Partly as a result of exposures by the Congressional committee and partly to let the pressure of accumulated charges subside, Renfroe left Alabama, supposedly for Texas. His absence

[12] *Ibid.*, I, Lewis E. Parsons, 101; Election Returns on file at the Department of Archives and History; John Witherspoon DuBose, *Alabama's Tragic Decade* . . . (Birmingham, 1940), 297; John Z. Sloan, "The Ku Klux Klan and the Alabama Election of 1872," *Alabama Review*, XVII (April, 1965), 120, brings new insights into the period.

[13] Sloan, "Ku Klux Klan and the Election of 1872," 115. Horn, *Invisible Empire*, 139. For comment on the Congressional committee's actions see Livingston *Journal*, November 10, 1871.

in 1872 was brief, and he was home again by 1873, although his activities were considerably curtailed.

In 1872 the Republicans resolved their internecine conflicts and made a united effort to recoup lost political ground. Backed by the Ku Klux Klan exposures, additional troops, election supervisors, and a United States marshal, Republican candidates campaigned hard. The Democrats were not able to generate much enthusiasm. At all levels—nationally, across the state, in Sumter County—the Republicans triumphed. Grant carried the state and David P. Lewis defeated Thomas H. Herndon, his Democratic opponent for governor. In Sumter County Lewis received 2,440 votes to Herndon's 1,733, a margin of 707.[14] Republicans were elected to county offices, as noted by Ben Herr's despairing comment in his *Journal*: "[Sumter County will be] represented in the lower house by three negroes who know no more about legislation—and have no more idea of political economy—than an oyster." [15]

Although the Klan was disbanded, in 1873 new terrorist orders such as the White League and the White Men's Association sprang into being. These groups never achieved the power or status of the Klan, but their existence was a final, if misguided, effort to redeem the state and county. With the important gubernational election of 1874 just ahead, Democrats readied themselves for a desperate struggle.

In Sumter County Renfroe was back and soon became the center of a controversy that reverberated across the state and attracted considerable national attention. It began with the mysterious murder of Walter P. Billings, a recently arrived carpetbagger.

---

[14] Returns on file at the Department of Archives and History; see also Livingston *Journal*, November 15, 1872.

[15] November 8, 1872.

CHAPTER VI

The Arrests

Walter P. Billings moved from New York to Sumter County late in 1873 or early in 1874. Originally from Missouri, he had lived in New York City for six years as a lawyer in a firm that was dissolved shortly before he came South. Billings was only thirty-two but the reason given for his move was his health. He made a down payment on a farm known as the Bruten place located on the tract of land called Grindstone Prairie in the county's northern section.

Although the Billings had no children, various relatives—among them Eugene Wells, a brother-in-law and former captain in the Union army—lived with them. Instead of devoting himself to agriculture, Billings formed a law partnership with Henry J. Greata, another Missouri native who migrated to Alabama in December 1873. Greata lived at Livingston, and, if he had a family, it remained in Missouri.

The firm of Billings & Greata, lodged in two rooms, one an office and the other a bedroom, was not overwhelmed with business, leaving the partners considerable time to devote to politics. Billings was especially active, attending Republican meetings and holding them at his home. He helped organize a political society among the Negroes known as the Friendly Brothers, soon rose to become chairman of the county Republican Executive Committee, and seemed a natural choice for the state legislature. On July 4, 1874, Billings, described only as "a recent

importation" presided over a convention in Livingston that
selected candidates for the crucial fall elections.[1] Billings also
acquired one-fourth interest in the Selma *Alabama State
Gazette*. This Republican paper was published by Emanuel H.
Saltiel, another Missourian who had helped persuade Billings to
move South.[2]

On August 1, which was a Saturday, Billings spoke to a
Republican convention at the Parker place, some eight or ten
miles from his home. As much social as political, the gathering
of Radicals was attended by Negroes and the leading white
Republicans. As Billings addressed the crowd, he allegedly
boasted that he had $10,000 (some said $5,000) with which to
carry the election and either slapped his thigh to indicate he had
the money with him or extracted a specimen bill to wave at the
audience. In either case, his listeners applauded wildly. Apparently Billings had obtained the money from state Republican
leaders at Montgomery, where he had been the previous week.[3]

Shortly after the speaking and the dinner that followed, a
Negro named Bob Ashford sought Billings out and informed
him that his wife was sick and wanted him to come home. Bor-
rowing a horse from his friend Alfred Wright, a Negro who
overheard Ashford's conversation, Billings departed but never
reached his destination. Just at sunset and within sight of his
home, Billings was ambushed and shot to death. A Negro discovered his body the next morning.

A jury of inquest, summoned by Acting Coroner J. E. Cusack,
traveled the nineteen miles from Livingston to the Bruten place.
The coroner's jury decreed the victim had been shot by an unknown person. Undertaker John H. Gray also went to Billings'
home and buried the body. Mrs. Billings did not attend the
funeral but remained with her brother at the home of a friend.

---

[1] Livingston *Journal*, July 10, 1874; *Select Committee on Affairs in
Alabama*, I (Washington, 1875), testimony of Thomas B. Wetmore, 939.

[2] *Affairs in Alabama*, Emanuel H. Saltiel, 1122, 1126.

[3] Montgomery *Alabama State Journal*, August 5, 1874; "Agricola," of
Coatopa to Mobile *Register*, August 6, 1874; Mobile *Register*, August 12,
1874, quoting Meridian *Mercury*; "Agrippa" to Mobile *Register*, August 18,
1874.

Juliette Billings wrote to a Masonic friend of her husbands's in New York, "I want to leave this dreadful country. . . . We were doing well with a fair crop when they killed him." [4] Within a few days she packed her belongings and departed.

Billings was scarcely buried before news of the crime created a furor. W. H. Wayne, Republican Clerk of the Circuit Court, wrote to Governor Lewis, "Mr. Billings had no personal enemies & his assassination must be accounted for on political grounds alone." Obviously shaken, Greata reported the murder to the governor and added, "Our lives are not safe here." [5] Greata left the county on the day Billings was buried.

As the news spread, reactions followed a predictable course. Governor Lewis offered the maximum reward of $400 and an attempt was made to raise $5,000 by private subscription.[6] Circuit Clerk Wayne's wife, who was the daughter of Probate Judge Abrahams, wrote influential Republicans in Washington requesting that troops be sent to Sumter County. Judge Abrahams feared he would be next to die and left for Washington to ask for soldiers.[7]

Even though Billings was a "mischief-making carpetbagger," the Meridian *Mercury* believed it "was a horrible thing to shoot a man down. . . ." [8] Democrats predicted that Republicans would convert the crime into a *cause celebre* and issued their own version of events: robbery was the motive. Because no pocketbook or money (except for a nickel discovered in a vest pocket) was found on Billings' body a Livingston paper speculated that Billings had been robbed. It was ironic, the Eutaw

[4] Livingston *Journal*, August 21, 1874, quoting Juliette W. Billings to New York *Sun;* Livingston *Journal*, August 7, 14, 1874; *Affairs in Alabama*, William H. Wayne, 663-664; Benjamin F. Herr, 685, disputed Mrs. Billings' claim with the statement that Billings was no farmer.

[5] W. H. Wayne to David P. Lewis, August 2, 1874, Governor's Correspondence; Henry J. Greata to David P. Lewis, Angust 2, 1874, *ibid.* The Lewis papers are on file at the Department of Archives and History.

[6] Montgormery *Alabama State Journal*, August 7, 1874.

[7] *Affairs in Alabama*, William H. Wayne, 663-665; James A. Abrahams, 763-766.

[8] Quoted in Mobile *Register*, August 8, 1874.

Whig and Observer noted, that Billings had been killed by the Negroes he had tried to help. "Agrippa," a Gainesville correspondent, argued that since Billings considered the white people of Sumter County friendly, motives other than theft should be ruled out.[9] A few days before the murder a Republican state official warned Billings to tone down any extreme speeches he had planned. Billings replied, "They have treated me very kindly; my neighbors have come to see me up to this time, and I do not think they are going to do any harm to me." [10]

Charges by Republican papers such as the Montgomery *State Journal* that the murder was politically inspired were denied by Democratic journals.[11]

What person or persons had killed Billings? The question was debated in the press, discussed in private, whispered on the streets. At Livingston, hotel manager D. W. Allen, a New Hampshire native and Union army veteran who had lived in Sumter five years, supposedly made statements reviving old stories of Renfroe as a Klansman and implicating him in the murder of Billings. It is doubtful whether the New Englander actually made the remarks, but Renfroe administered a beating to Allen in the street fronting the hotel.

Young Addison G. Smith, a twenty-three-year-old lawyer who saw the fight, was asked several months later to describe Renfroe. He told the Congressional committee, "Mr. Renfroe is as nice a gentleman as I know of. He is quick-tempered." Smith admitted that Renfroe had been in a lot of unnecessary trouble, but as for the fight with Allen, "I say that 'most any man will be incensed at a charge of that kind." But was fighting in the street the proper way for a quiet, peaceable man to act? "I did not say he was the most quiet. I said he was the nicest gentleman I know of. I said furthermore, that he was quick tempered. I will say, too that when a man gets into a personal

---

[9] Livingston *Journal*, August 7, 1874; quoted in Mobile *Register* August 18, 1874; "Agrippa" to Mobile *Register*, August 18, 1874.

[10] *Affairs in Alabama*, James G. Stokes, 1070. Dr. William A. Jones, a Republican, 644, and William H. Wayne, 668, both testified that Billings was a quiet, respectable, educated man who had no political enemies.

[11] Mobile *Register*, August 16, 1874; Livingston *Journal*, August 21, 1874; Montgomery *Alabama State Journal*, August 5, 1874.

difficulty, it does not injure him in my estimation, if he defends himself." A man should not attack another without provocation, but "It does not hurt a man, in my estimation, to defend his own character." [12]

Thomas B. Wetmore, an influential lawyer, also saw the struggle. Wetmore thought Renfroe went too far, adding that he had been drinking (although this was the only time he had seen Renfroe even slightly intoxicated). Was Renfroe not a violent man? "I have not been with him often and don't know his habits as to violence," Wetmore testified. "I understand that he is a man of irritable disposition and quick to resent an insult." Yet he did not know that Renfroe had threatened to kill Allen. Moreover, "I have never seen him except when he appeared to be courteous and gentlemanly. I have never seen him show this irritation I speak of, but have understood he was a man quick to resent an insult." [13]

There were others who saw the affray and testified. Nothing came of the affair, and Allen, a registered Democrat, wrote in the local paper that Renfroe was "activated by the belief that I had accused him of a crime that I really did not believe him guilty of." Despite this statement one Radical paper charged that certain parties in Livingston bought Renfroe a new coat for thrashing Allen.[14]

No one was more insistent on seeing justice done in the Billings case than the quadroon Thomas L. Ivey. Supposedly the son of a Sumter County planter, Ivey had been sent North to Philadelphia before the war for his education. Ivey's private life (he was married and had a child who died) attracted little notice, but his public proclamations made him well known. His maledictions against the whites were so strident that the Republicans refused to nominate him for office. A prominent white Republican said Ivey was "a very tumultuous man—a very im-

---

[12] *Affairs in Alabama*, 876.

[13] *Ibid.*, 940-941.

[14] *Ibid.*, Benjamin F. Herr, 683; Alfred Wright (Negro), 559; Emanuel H. Saltiel, 1129. Livingston *Journal*, September 4, 1874, contained Allen's note and printed but denied charges of the Montgomery *Alabama State Journal*, August 27, 1874.

prudent man. . . . He was oppressive in his talk, speech and
action." In short, "I think he was the worst colored man I ever
knew in the district, the very worst." [15] When Ivey was not
threatening to enter politics, he taught school. Finally, with the
aid of Congressman Hays, he got a job as mail agent on the
Alabama and Chattanooga Railroad.

Continuing to issue his vitriolic statements, Ivey became the
most hated Negro in the county. The Negro Bob Reed, a more
temperate man who served in the state legislature, had assumed
a place of real power among the Negroes, but the mercurial Ivey
was widely feared. As early as 1872 it was reported "A saddle-
colored freeman named Ivey . . . has for some time made himself offensively officious. . . ." [16] By 1874 Ivey maintained a
bodyguard that fluctuated from twenty-five to estimates of over
one hundred men.

On the day Billings was killed and at least once afterwards,
Ivey spoke to large gatherings of Negroes at Coatopa. Ivey supposedly appeared in Livingston with a double-barreled shotgun
and issued a threat: "Show me the man who shot Billings, and
I'll shoot his damned head off." [17] About this time he wrote to
Governor Lewis requesting protection. Mentioning the necessity
for a bodyguard, Ivey asked, "Cant we be protected by the
proper authority [?] Please let me hear from you as soon as you
get this." [18]

On the afternoon of August 29, the westbound Alabama and
Chattanooga train was about three miles north of York station
when Engineer Charlie Biggs spotted a Negro man standing on
the track and waiving his hat. Sparks flew from the wheels as
the train ground to an unscheduled stop. A Negro eyewitness,
twenty-four-year-old James Brown, said later that he saw a

[15] *Affairs in Alabama*, Dr. William B. Jones, 645; Jones added that
Congressman Hays did not like Ivey; Benjamin F. Herr, 677, said that
Greata did not approve of Ivey either.

[16] Livingston *Journal*, November 15, 1872; *Affairs in Alabama*, James
Brown, 504-505; for Ivey's background see Addison G. Smith, 869.

[17] Thomas Ivey to David P. Lewis, August 5, 1874, Governor's Correspondence; see also Livingston *Journal*, August 21, 1874.

[18] "Gana" from Coatopa to Mobile *Register*, September 2, 1874.

dozen men hidden in a drain near the trestle open fire. The men were on both sides of the track. The target of the buckshot charged guns was Ivey. He was hit and killed instantly. Mission completed, the men disappeared into the woods.

Ivey's body was carried to Meridian, but was later brought back to Coatopa. There a large crowd of Negroes—some angry, others commenting that they expected it to happen—viewed the remains. No inquest was held, and he was buried at Livingston. One Democratic editor believed Ivey's public sneers and pronouncements had "foolishly and needlessly provoked his fate." [19] Another pointed out that with the election at hand, the last thing Democrats wanted was to be charged with a political murder. The journalist claimed many Negroes looked on Ivey as "an insolent, incendiary character." [20]

Nothing could erase the glaring fact that within a month, two men, both Republicans, had met violent deaths. On September 7, a public meeting of native whites at the Livingston courthouse denounced the murders and repudiated all forms of lawlessness. A similar meeting at the village of Intercourse also stated its opposition to violence. Republicans charged that both men had been Ku-Kluxed. While failure to lament the deaths of Billings and Ivey extended beyond the perpetrators of the crimes, most people in the county determined to have the guilty persons brought to justice. To this end efforts to solve the crimes were intensified.[21]

At Washington one cabinet officer, Attorney General George H. Williams, was bombarded with written and verbal requests to take action. He responded on September 3, by sending to Robert W. Healy, United States marshal for the Southern Dis-

[19] Mobile *Register*, September 2, 1874, quoting Meridian *Mercury;* see also "Gana" to Mobile *Register*, September 2, 1874. For a bitter account of Ivey's murder see Montgomery *Alabama State Journal*, September 1, 2, 1874. See also *Affairs in Alabama*, James Brown, 503-509; J. R. Larkin, 660; and Meridian *Mercury*, August 30, 1874, quoted 1220-1221.

[20] Livingston *Journal*, September 4, 1874; *Affairs in Alabama*, William B. Jones, 644, although a Republican, said Ivey was killed because of his bad behavior.

[21] *Affairs in Alabama*, Benjamin F. Herr, 674-677.

trict of Alabama, instructions to move vigorously in carrying out the Enforcement Acts. From his headquarters at Montgomery, Healy was directed "to proceed, with all possible energy and dispatch to detect, expose, arrest, and punish" persons guilty of crimes denying citizens of their constitutional rights.[22]

Federal authority as represented by Captain William Mills, two other officers, and the thirty-two enlisted men of Company A of the Second Infantry arrived at Livingston on September 11. They set up camp on the courthouse square, treating the citizens to the unusual sight of army tents dotted across the green. Captain Mills was nothing if not vigilant. Guards were posted in the traditional manner, and at night the men in the tents were required to keep their clothes and belts on and their weapons loaded.[23]

The military was present to maintain order in Livingston and throughout the county. More surreptitious means were employed to investigate the murders of Billings and Ivey. The stakes were high because, if the murders had been committed to intimidate Negroes and Radicals, then the acts would achieve this purpose if the guilty remained free. Aside from the obvious need to uphold the law, there remained the necessity of convincing Republicans they were safe in voting for the candidates of their choice. To achieve this, four unusual men appeared in Sumter County. Two of them, G. B. Randolph and J. O. Williford, were deputy United States marshals. Ordered to Livingston by Healy, they disguised themselves as privates in Captain Mills' company and took part in routine military duty.

Far more devious were Joseph G. Hester, a detective of the Post Office Department, and Josiah N. Beach, a government agent of the Treasury Department, who was investigating internal revenue matters as well as murders. Accompanied by a driver (a man named Keith who had no official capacity), the two men appeared in Livingston on September 21, riding in a

---

[22] *Ibid.,* George H. Williams, 1218-1223, 1264.

[23] *Ibid.,* Captain William Mills, 1946-1047, 1060. See also NA Publications, Microcopy 666 Rolls 169-173. These rolls, on file at the National Archives, reproduce file 357790 AGO 1874. See William Mills to Assistant Adjutant General, September 22, 1874, Roll 170, RG 94.

canvass-covered prairie schooner drawn by a pair of bareboned mules. The men, dressed in jeans and cowhide boots, claimed to be from Nash County, North Carolina. Their wagon contained manufactured tobacco, but, more important, a cargo of apple brandy and whiskey. Setting up shop in a little grove outside town, the men obtained a license to sell, and quickly ingratiated themselves with the townspeople. The imposters had a drink at the town's only saloon, had their pictures taken, and returned to their camp, where they put up a rough board on which was bespattered in ill-shaped letters the words:

Tobaco and Whiskey
For Sail Hear

Soon the personable tarheels were recounting their exploits as members of the Ku Klux Klan in North Carolina. According to his own report, Hester was well received by the people. Hester was primarily concerned with finding the men who killed Ivey. Indefatigable and ubiquitous, Hester said on one occasion, 'I would arrest the President of the United States if I had a warrant for him." (A Sumter County woman who was no admirer of Grant, told Hester she wished he would). In most situations Hester did the talking. Beach explained his silence: "I had some talking to do, but when it was a very tough crowd I did not have much to say, for my particular Yankee twang I was afraid they would detect, and he being a southern man could pass pretty well." [24]

Since the investigators' findings revealed several men had taken part in the murders, particularly that of Billings, the problem of arresting them was difficult. Separate captures would alert others who would undoubtedly flee. Late in September, almost two months after Billings' death, Randolph and Williford were summoned in from their daily drill with the other soldiers. Hester had called a hurried conference because, as the purveyor of liquors explained, an excellent opportunity to

[24] Chicago *Inter Ocean*, October 5, 9, 15, 1874; Montgomery *Alabama State Journal*, October 8, 1874; *Affairs in Alabama*, Joseph G. Hester, 1011, 1007-1009; G. B. Randolph, 500; Josiah N. Beach, 39, 1186-1190, 1192.

capture the suspects had come up. On Monday, September 28, the Democrats were scheduled to hold their county nominating convention at the Livingston Courthouse. Beach was out of town and Hester would not participate in the arrests, but apparently it was he who devised the plan. At all events, the convention seemed the ideal time and place to strike.

Affidavits based on charges by the Negro Alfred Wright had already been signed and warrants issued by United States Commissioner James Gillette at Mobile. It was decided to permit the convention to proceed normally through the day and spring the trap that night. The courthouse would be ringed with soldiers who could apprehend any fugitives who might slip through the hands of Randolph and his assistants when they made a bold entry into the meeting.[25]

Some two or three hundred Democratic delegates and spectators gathered at the courthouse on the appointed day and went through the spirited paces of selecting their ticket. The gathering was a rollicking social event but was attended by men determined to name a slate of candidates who could win. That evening between eight and nine o'clock as the meeting was casting its thirty-fourth ballot in an extended contest to nominate a probate judge, the federal officials marched into the hall. Randolph, Williford, and a Lieutenant L. S. Ames looked across a room of startled hostile faces. Suddenly raucous shouts were replaced by absolute silence.

In the abrupt quiet, everybody present listened as Randolph's voice cut like a knife through the semi-lit room: "Mr. Chairman, I have a United States warrant for the arrest of persons whom I suppose are in this building. If you will suspend your proceedings for a few moments it will oblige me very much." [26]

Randolph followed his statement with a warning that the courthouse was surrounded by soldiers and escape was impossible. He named Renfroe, Charles H. Bullock, M. P. (Mark)

---

[25] Chicago *Inter Ocean*, October 9, 1874.

[26] *Ibid.*, October 5, 1874; Livingston *Journal*, October 2, 1874; Mobile *Register*, October 3, 1874, quoting "Grattan." For various eyewitness accounts of the arrests see *Affairs in Alabama*, James D. Williford, 430; Thomas B. Wetmore, 918; Benjamin F. Herr, 679.

Sledge, and seven other men. The convention chairman examined the papers carefully before helping to point out the accused. Sheriff Samuel Williamson also gave reluctant but timely assistance.

Bullock, described by a Radical reporter as a "tall, slouch-looking man, whose shoulders were set on a level with his ears, and whose carrot-colored head was poised at a painful angle," was present as a delegate. He was quickly taken into custody. The reporter noted Bullock's long arms and large hands and concluded "his whole attitude [was] that of a man who has habitually leaned against a post." [27] A more charitable description placed the thin Bullock in his thirties and commented on his light colored hair and whiskers.[28]

The easiest man to spot, although he was present as a spectator and not as a delegate, was Renfroe. The reporter who supplied the unflattering description of Bullock, said of Renfroe, "From appearances, Renfroe is a man whom you would distrust. Huguet 'bowed too low,' but Renfroe does not bow at all. He shoves along without doing anyone obeisance. He takes no notice of kindness and never speaks except to curse some one." No mistaking him, "everybody in Sumter knows Steve Renfroe. . . ." [29]

Randolph searched Renfroe but found nothing except a small penknife. After assurances from Williford he would not be harmed, Renfroe was marched out of the courthouse. Outside four armed soldiers were waiting. According to Renfroe, Williford told the soldiers, "Take this tiger, and if he attempts to get away shoot him." Renfroe said he was then marched to a tent, seated on a bunk, and told by an Orderly Sergeant, who leveled his gun at him, "if you move, hand, foot or finger, I'll blow the top of your head off." [30] Renfroe did not move.

Bullock soon joined him and received similar threats. The two prisoners were handcuffed and taken to the county jail. The handcuffs stayed on, and the men claimed, although it was later

27 Chicago *Inter Ocean*, October 9, 1874.
28 Mobile *Register*, October 9, 1874.
29 Chicago *Inter Ocean*, October 9, 1874.
30 Livingston *Journal*, October 16, 1874, quoting Mobile *Register*.

denied, they were also chained together. Their stay in the Livingston jail would last until Friday morning.[31]

Back at the courthouse the marshals and soldiers continued their attempts to find the other men named in the warrants. The dimly illuminated hall impeded their efforts, but they were helped by one shadowy figure with a candle who walked among the people calling the name of Mark Sledge. After trying to find Sledge inside, he abandoned his efforts and was permitted by the soldiers to seek him on the courthouse grounds. Once outside it was an easy matter to blow out the candle and disappear. In this way, Mark Sledge deceived the federal officers, and by appearing to look for himself, made good his escape.[32]

With the knowledge that federal officers and detectives were searching through the county making arrests, several whites who either took part in the crimes or were afraid of being falsely accused fled the county. Zach Tutt, one of the men for whom a warrant was issued, was visited at his home on Tuesday night (he had not been present at the Monday convention). Tutt made a desperate dash out his back door and escaped across the swamps. Soldiers fired at him but missed and had to content themselves with capturing four shotguns.[33]

W. L. (Fred) Chiles, one of the men James Brown claimed to have seen when Ivey was killed, was not so fortunate. A former deputy sheriff, Chiles was twenty-six and "a real sensible looking fellow." Chiles was just closing up the gristmill where he worked when Hester and Deputy Marshal Randolph arrested him. He was placed in a wagon and carried along in a fruitless search for one Alonzo Kornegay, still another man implicated by Brown in the Ivey murder. Afterward Chiles was handcuffed and placed in jail with Renfroe and Bullock. It would later be charged that in attempting to locate Kornegay, Hester had im-

[31] *Ibid.*

[32] Montgomery *Alabama State Journal*, October 4, 1874; Mobile *Register*, October 2, 1874, quoting Meridian *Mercury;* Chicago *Inter Ocean*, October 9, 1874.

[33] For accounts sympathetic to the Republican and Billings viewpoint see daily rpeorts during the first two weeks in October in the Chicago *Inter Ocean*.

pressed private citizens into action, searched private homes, and detained innocent people against their will.[34]

All of those arrested were charged with having violated the recently passed Enforcement Acts. One Radical Mobile paper was pleased to see what it claimed was a reversal of roles, while the Florence *Republican* was delighted that "Steve Renfroe and Chas. Bullock, two of the infamous assassins of Walter P. Billings, were captured. . . ."[35]

The most unusual aspect of the frenzied arrests and escapes was the apparent docility of Renfroe. Why had he surrendered so tamely, and why, in light of what would happen in the future, did he make no attempt to escape? One important clue to his out-of-character behavior came in testimony before a Congressional committee in January 1875. Duncan Dew, Jr., a commission merchant in Greene County, was a Democrat but also handled the business affairs of Republican Congressman Hays. Dew said Hays told him a warrant was going to be served on Renfroe and wanted the businessman to warn Renfroe in time for him to leave the county. Hays gave assurances that all past charges would be dropped if Renfroe left. Although Hays' motives were difficult to explain, Dew made certain contacts and Renfroe received the proposal. He refused to depart. He had left once, he said, but not now. Renfroe protested that since he was innocent he would not run. Dew said a highly respected citizen told him Renfroe "had been a law abiding gentleman; and had married a nice lady; and other people gave me the same statement."[36] It does not seem likely that Dew fabricated his testimony, although Hays never commented one way or the other concerning the episode. If the event actually occurred, then Renfroe knew he would be arrested and either was innocent or did not believe he would be convicted.

Although federal officials justified their actions as necessary, Sumter County citizens and others had a different interpreta-

---

[34] Chicago *Inter Ocean*, October 9, 1874; Mobile *Register*, October 10, 1874, quoting letter to an unidentified Montgomery newspaper. *Affairs in Alabama*. W. F. Chiles, 747; James Brown, 503-504.

[35] Chicago *Inter Ocean*, October 27, 1874, quoting Mobile *Watchman*.

[36] *Affairs in Alabama*, Duncan Dew, Jr., 541-542.

tion. They soon charged that since the warrants were issued on September 28, the entire affair was politically motivated. The arrests, they asserted, were designed to cause the maximum amount of political embarrassment to the Democrats. Editor Herr of the *Journal* wrote, "the probability is that the prisoners will soon be restored to liberty; for as we believe, nothing short of the basest perjury can connect them with the commission of that crime." He added, "Believing that they are guiltless, the unfortunate men have the sympathy of the community." [37]

The Mobile *Register* headed one editorial denouncing the arrests as an invasion of personal liberty with the caption "The United States Government Ku-Kluxing." The *Register* believed "The time and manner of the arrest is for political effect." The truth was "that Billings was murdered for the money he claimed to have on his person, that Ivey was murdered because he was a dangerous and turbulent man, who had ridden through the streets of a peaceable village threatening to visit it with fire and blood." [38] The Meridian *Mercury*'s editor, furious at the invasion by bayonets, warned, "If right ever get the better of might again, there may be a day of reckoning for that Livingston outrage." Leaving matters to a higher power, a Tuscaloosa editor wrote, "God only knows how this people can tamely submit to such unprovoked degradation and injury." [39]

Republicans and their spokesmen were firmly convinced of the prisoners' guilt. Despite a formal denial by the Democratic State Executive Committee, Congressman Hays charged that the Sumter crimes, as well as others, were attempts at political intimidation.[40] "Verily, 'murder will out,' " one Radical editor declared.[41] The Montgomery *State Journal* charged Renfroe with being a "notorious KuKlux leader" and insisted "that the killing

[37] October 2, 1874; see *ibid.*, October 9, 1874, quoting Montgomery *News*.

[38] October 2, 3, 1874; for similar sentiments and a direct appeal to President Grant to intervene, see *ibid.*, October 7, 1874, quoting Meridian *Mercury*.

[39] Quoted in Mobile *Register*, October 3, 1874; Tuscaloosa *Blade*, October 15, 1874.

[40] Mobile *Register*, October 7, 1874.

[41] Florence *Republican*, October 6, 1874.

of Billings, on account of his politics, was not the first murder that he was ever engaged in!" The same paper predicted, Renfroe "will doubtless swing for his participation in the murder of Billings, if not for other crimes." So would Bullock. "If therefore Steve Renfroe is a 'gentle man,' then the term seems to have been prostituted to simply mean an out-law in Sumter, and does not describe the character, which is usually covered by the term in other sections of the United States." [42] From Jefferson City, Missouri, Mrs. Billings wrote Hester castigating the men who killed her husband and declaring "Renfroe was also one of them, and if he escapes it will be simply because there is no such thing as justice in the South." [43] Several times the Chicago *Inter Ocean* called Renfroe a "Kluklux assassin," a "political desperado . . . defended by the most respectable Democratic newspapers of Alabama," and "the terror of Sumter County." [44]

That neither side would accept any arguments presented by the other was obvious. Although the men had only been arrested, one Republican paper alleged that the murder had been plotted at Sledge's home and Renfroe had fired the first shot. A Democrat journal was equally convinced Renfroe and the others were "arrested, not for crime . . . but to strike terror into the white people of the section in which they live, and to add to the chances of the success of the Radical party." [45]

Like everything else connected with the Billings case, the removal of the prisoners from Livingston to Mobile for a hearing provoked bitter controversy. For one thing, why they were carried three hundred miles to Mobile when there was a United States commissioner in Livingston was never made clear. What happened on the way to Mobile, of course, had two versions, but as related by the prisoners, they were awakened at four o'clock on Friday morning, October 2. They were told they were being taken to Coatopa station, ten miles from Livingston. The pre-

---

[42] October 4, 6, 14, 1874.

[43] *Affairs in Alabama,* 690, quoting letter from Juliette W. Billings to J. G. Hester, October 13, 1874.

[44] See issues of October 8, 12, 1874.

[45] Montgomery *Alabama State Journal,* October 6, 1874; Mobile *Register,* October 3, 1874.

dawn removal was contrary to the promises of Marshals Randolph and Williford, who had assured the prisoners of sufficient notice to enable them to see their families and get some clothing. Randolph told them later he would have notified their counsel had there been a trustworthy person in Sumter County. Renfroe's wife would soon have a baby, and while the uncertainties of the hearing and the separation were difficult, it is unlikely that Renfroe permitted his anxiety to show.

Loaded into a strongly guarded four-horse covered wagon, the party of prisoners and guards proceeded about five miles from Livingston, where it was joined by two soldiers, Detective Hester, and two Negro witnesses (one of them Alfred Wright). After some conversation the groups separated with the witnesses joining the party. Hester did not go to Mobile. Instead of going to Coatopa, the marshals took the prisoners toward Demopolis. While resting at Belmont, six miles from Demopolis, the group encountered one P. A. Hillman who rode up and asked Renfroe, apparently in all innocence, where he was going. Renfroe said he did not know and responded to Hillman's inquiries about ginning cotton and his financial condition.

The stocky Hillman, a young man of twenty-five with auburn colored hair and whiskers, offered to go home, get some seed cotton, and sell it to raise money for Renfroe. Randolph objected to the conversation and cut it off. As Hillman rode off, Randolph asked him if his name was Billy Hillman. It was his nickname, Hillman replied, and was quickly informed that he was under arrest. A Negro soldier had told Randolph the talkative Southerner was Billy Hillman. His naturally florid complexion reddened as Hillman demanded that Randolph produce a warrant. The marshal said one was not necessary, although he brought out a piece of paper which he never unfolded. Hillman was handcuffed and chained to the wagon alongside Chiles. In desperation he told the marshals that his cousin was named William Hillman. Randolph replied, "It don't make a damn bit of difference, we'll take you along now and get him some other time."

At Demopolis the prisoners, still handcuffed and chained, were put in a tent and placed under strong guard. The sergeant told the sentinels to shoot the prisoners if they attempted to escape. They remained overnight at Demopolis, and the next morning were marched under guard to the depot and put on the train for Selma. The prisoners maintained that on the train and for the entire trip, meals were always ordered for two while they did without.

When the party reached Selma the prisoners were marched to jail, but their route was partially blocked by a crowd of angry blacks. The former bondsmen were understandably hostile toward the whites and made their sentiments vocal by referring to the Sumter County men as Ku Kluxers. The men were kept in jail at Selma for two hours before being placed on the train for Montgomery.

At Benton, a large group of Negroes who had just adjourned a political meeting was waiting at the depot. They boarded the train and converged on both doors of the prisoners' car but could not gain entrance. Renfroe and his companions were denounced, called Ku-Kluxers, and taunted with prophecies that all would be found guilty. The blacks also made known their approval of civil rights, some of them staying on the train until it reached Manack. There they got off and marched alongside the prisoners' car shouting and making threats.

Renfroe told Randolph if he could not defend them to take his handcuffs off and unchain him so that he could protect himself. Williford drew his pistol and said, "I have an idea to turn you out among them. If you don't take your seat and be quiet I'll shoot you." As the train started, Randolph pulled out a small derringer and fired it out of the window into the ground. Undaunted, the Negroes continued their demonstrations chasing the train until it was out of sight.[46] A Montgomery paper reported the scene at Manack as as "unusual degradation and cruel exposure," and "harsh and barbarous treatment. . . ." [47]

[46] The story of their journey to Mobile was related to a Mobile *Register* reporter who visited the prisoners in their cell. See that paper October 6, 7, 1874; for a description of Hillman see *ibid.*, October 7, 1874. See also *Affairs in Alabama*, Deputy Williford, 746-747, who said, "We were treated pretty shabbily all the way there."

[47] Mobile *Register*, October 6, 1874, quoting Montgomery *News*.

When the train reached Montgomery, it was met by another group of Negroes who followed the prisoners from the depot to the jail where Randolph made them disperse. At Montgomery the prisoners got a good meal, which they assumed was sent them by friends in the city, but otherwise were not treated well. "H. C.," a correspondent for the New York *Times*, inspected the cell in which they were placed and declared that it was so filthy the men could not lie down; it was small, close and coffin-like, built entirely of stone. The room was four feet wide, eight feet long, six feet high and two feet underground. It was ventilated by a small hole cut in its iron door. The men had neither beds nor blankets.[48]

A caustic Republican editor in the capital city wrote, "Unfortunately our jail here in Montgomery was not got up to suit the fastidious tastes of these bad men! But then it is so rare that a white murderer ever gets into our jail, and these Sumter murderers were such unexpected guests, that the mere fact that everything was not to their liking, ought to be overlooked." [49]

The next day the prisoners were paraded through the streets again and placed on the train for Mobile. The party of prisoners, detectives, soldiers, and witnesses reached Mobile on Sunday, October 4. It was late in the evening and there was no food at the county jail, so Randolph and Williford ordered supper from a restaurant (paying for the food, according to one report, out of their own pockets). The jail was a comfortable one, and the prisoners, to understate the case, were well treated.

Marshals Williford and Randolph took vigorous exception to the particulars of the trip from Livingston to Mobile as related by the prisoners to the Mobile *Register* and copied across the country. The marshals claimed the published accounts were false. They were, the officers insisted, careful to provide their charges with good food; there were no crowds of Negroes who insulted the prisoners. As for the secretive exodus from Livingston, the prisoners were arrested on Monday night but were not removed until Friday morning. This should have been sufficient

---

48 Quoted in Mobile *Register,* October 30, 1874.
49 Montgomery *Alabama State Journal,* October 8, 1874.

time for them to get ready. The early departure and circuitous route were employed because suspicious characters began gathering about the jail, and the marshals feared a rescue would be attempted. They claimed to have been done a gross injustice simply because they did their job and accomplished their mission.

"We had unpleasant duties to perform," they wrote, "and we discharged them with kindness and consideration to those whom we arrested; and we brought our prisoners *safely* to the jail at Mobile." [50] A Northern reporter who accompanied the party from Montgomery upheld the marshals' story. The prisoners were given good food, tobacco, and papers to read. They were not chained, merely handcuffed, and in general were well treated. A bitter Williford, disturbed by references to himself and Randolph as "two infernal minions of despotism," said later, "If a man does anything for the United States government he is looked upon with about as favorable eyes as Gabriel looked upon the devil in paradise." [51]

During the next few days Renfroe and his companions were visited by crowds of sympathizers, who, in addition to wishing them well, were said to have furnished them bedding, mosquito bars, underclothing, dainty edibles, and even wines. A Mobile paper hoped the prisoners would be provided for physically and receive from the city's bar "the finest talent and the warmest zeal of the profession." [52] Support for the prisoners was so manifest that a Chicago reporter said, "I have not met a single white man, outside of the Radical Club here, who does not sympathize with the prisoners, and declares their innocence. . . ." [53]

---

[50] *Ibid.*, October 14, 1874, quoting letter of the marshals to Mobile *Register*. The prisoners also wrote a note clearing up, or attempting to clear up, the circumstances of their being brought to Mobile. For criticism of the detectives see Tuscaloosa *Blade*, October 15, 1874. For Captain William Mills' versions of the arrests see his report to Assistant Adjutant General, October 14, 1874, Roll 170, RG 94, National Archives.

[51] Chicago *Inter Ocean*, October 9, 1874; *Affairs in Alabama*, James D. Williford, 433.

[52] Mobile *Register*, October 6, 1874.

[53] Chicago *Inter Ocean*, October 7, 1874.

Mobile's overwhelming concern with the market prices of cotton was temporarily forgotten. The forthcoming hearing for Renfroe and the Sumter County men had displaced the fleecy staple as the main topic of conversation.

CHAPTER VII

The Hearing

The hearing began at 11 A.M. on Tuesday morning, October 6, as the prisoners were arraigned before United States Commissioner James Gillette. Thus began what was called "one of the most singular judicial proceedings which ever occurred under the flag of a civilized nation." [1]

An admirer wrote that Commissioner Gillette, a small young man with blond hair and mustache, had lines "around his mouth that spell firmness." Representing the United States was District Attorney George M. Duskin, assisted by W. W. D. Turner. Also on hand to aid the prosecution was Lieutenant Governor Alexander McKinstry.

The prisoners were defended by several of the state's most able lawyers: A. W. Cockrell of Sumter County, R. H. & R. I. Smith of Mobile, and John Little Smith and Thomas Herndon of Mobile. Herndon had been the unsuccessful Democratic candidate for governor in 1872. A reporter at the hearing commented, "The attorneys for defense are Southern gentlemen of the old school. They say 'I reckon,' and 'where were you at?' and their voices have that broad accent that is common to their class." [2]

Whites and Negroes packed the courtroom. The Negroes, undoubtedly hostile to the prisoners but judiciously silent, sat on

[1] Mobile *Register*, October 6, 1874.
[2] "Curtis" writing in Chicago *Inter Ocean*, October 12, 1874. See also Mobile *Register*, October 7, 1874.

one side while the whites, strongly sympathetic to the accused, occupied the other side. Witnesses for the prosecution were put in the grand jury room; those favorable to the prisoners waited in the petit jury room.

Renfroe dominated the gathering. Although he would not utter a word during the trial, a journalist was awed by his "prepossessing appearance." Another writer remarked, "Renfroe sat through the trial without showing a single sign of emotion, or even interest." Silent, occupied with inward thoughts, Renfroe made his presence felt as much as seen.[3]

Henry J. Greata, Billings' law partner, was the first witness for the prosecution. He testified he had known Billings for two years. Greata had last seen his legal associate alive on July 29, at a Republican convention at Uniontown. They had separated after the meeting with Greata going to Meridian. Greata returned to Billings' home on Thursday (July 30) where he remained until Sunday, August 2. He was inside the house on the evening of the murder and stated that between sundown and dusk he heard the sounds of guns being fired. He assumed they were the shots that killed Billings, although he did not actually see the body until the next morning. On cross-examination Greata pointed out his relationship with Billings was as his law partner and that they cultivated no land together.

Confused but damaging testimony was given by Richard Wright, a Negro boy who described himself as "going on 17." Wright had been employed as a field hand since January 1874 by his uncle, John Little. Wright said he had known Renfroe and Bullock for five years (he did not know Hillman). The week before the shooting the boy had heard of a dinner being held at Ramsey's Station (located about two or three miles from Billings' house). Although he had no invitation, Wright said, "I was free privileged and could go where I pleased." He left Friday evening, traveling by signboards and vague directions. After spending Friday night with a man named Andrew Simms, he started out again on Saturday.

---

[3] Mobile *Register*, October 7, 1874; Chicago *Inter Ocean*, October 7, 1874.

The Negro youth never got to the dinner because about two miles from Ramsey's Station he met Nelson Doyle, a Negro described by the boy as an old man. Doyle, lowering a haversack of tools from his back, asked Wright if he knew where there was any work. The lad replied that he did, and, after the older man told him the dinner at Ramsey's Station was over, the two turned around. Wright agreed to let Doyle stay at his father's place, a farm owned by the widow Branch. Their meeting was scarely more than a hundred yards from Billings' house.

At this time, "about a half hour by the sun," they saw Billings approaching on a horse belonging to Wright's father. When Billings got within fifty or sixty yards, the Negro said he saw Renfroe spring up out of the woods where he had been hiding. With a pistol in his hand Renfroe approached Billings and said in loud tones, "Halt! God damn you." Billings refused to stop, and then in the words of Wright, "four or five other men rose up and shot Billings down." The other men had double-barreled shotguns. According to Wright, "when the shots were fired both Billings and the horse fell dead."

The boy mentioned several other men who were present, including Bullock but not Hillman. He did not know whether Billings or his horse had been killed first but recalled hearing several shots fired and seeing five or six guns. Questioned more closely, Wright increased the number of men to twenty or twenty-five, adding that he saw no horses.

Renfroe advanced on Wright and Doyle, who stood rigid with fear. Renfroe told Doyle, "Old man, God damn you, get out of this country." Wright said that the Negro complied, instantly breaking through the woods.

Renfroe also ordered Wright to leave Sumter County, but the boy protested that he had no money. Renfroe then gave Wright $20 in bills with instructions to report to him the next morning. Then the assassins quickly departed in the direction taken by Doyle, and Wright went home to his uncle's, passing by the body of Billings and the dead horse. Instead of meeting Renfroe, Wright left Sumter County on Monday morning for Meridian. He departed early without telling his uncle of his plans. The

Negro boy had never been to Meridian, and was accompanied by William Lee, a young friend. They reached the Mississippi town on Wednesday morning, August 5.

Wright kept his secret for two weeks, but after his father finally contacted him the youth recounted what he had witnessed. He did not return to Sumter County. Instead, his father brought him from Meridian to Mobile, where he had been six or seven weeks. They came by train, but Wright was uncertain about where his father got the money to pay their fare. The defense asked Wright if his father told him why he had been brought to Mobile, but the prosecution's objection was sustained. The Negro had been working on the streets of Mobile, although he did not know who got him the job. If the testimony of a seventeen-year-old Negro boy was accepted, then Renfroe and his companions were in serious difficulty.[4]

Next to testify for the prosecution was Nelson Doyle. His testimony, as well as that of other witnesses, was reported in the press in vivid "local color," with the reporters providing what they considered verbatim quotations complete with phonetic spelling. Compared to Doyle, Wright's appearance was a study in clarity. Doyle was described by a Mobile reporter as "A swift witness, swift on foot and swift of tongue; one who recognizes Divine dispensation in all things. . . ." The forty-five-year-old Negro was at the same time crafty and ingenuous, confused and clear, and, above all, an incredibly entertaining witness.

Doyle said he was from Uniontown, Perry County, but had been a laborer for a white man in Mississippi earlier in the year. In March he went to Meridian and from there he came to Sumter County looking for carpentry work. On the Saturday of Billings' murder he met a man and talked about possible employment. Later in the day he met Richard Wright. Doyle confirmed the boy's story about the meeting in the road and their starting toward the house of Wright's father.

[4] Mobile *Register*, October 7, 1874, ran almost complete accounts of the testimony. *Affairs in Alabama*, Richard Wright, 556-558, contains an expansion of his remarks.

Although he had heard of Billings, Doyle had never seen him until Wright said "Yonder comes Mr. Billings on my father's horse." Doyle did not know Bullock or Renfroe but had seen them both before. The Negro related essentially the same story as Wright but added there were twenty-five or thirty men and that he saw eight or ten horses saddled and hitched in the woods about seventy yards back. He recognized Zach Tartt, Billy Hillman, and some others, including Bullock and Renfroe.

After the shooting, Doyle remembered his thoughts: "We are dead, we are dead." Young Wright cautioned him not to run, but once Renfroe dismissed him, Doyle went across the woods until he came to a Negro's house four miles away. He could have obtained work but left because he was afraid to remain. The witness admitted telling Bob Reed and "some Radical people in the neighborhood" about the murder. Some three weeks later he went to work for Billy Hillman (itself an amazing act since he had supposedly seen Hillman at the scene of the crime).

While in Hillman's employ, Doyle was visited at night by a group of white men who took him out and whipped him. Among those administering the beating was Zach Tartt, owner of a cream colored horse. Doyle apparently suddenly remembered seeing such an animal tied in the woods near the spot of Billings' murder and concluded that the parties who whipped him were those who shot Billings. Because his employer, Hillman, also participated in the whipping, Doyle belatedly remembered his involvement in the murder. Was he sure he had not associated Hillman with the murder until the night he was whipped? "Certain as God made Moses," Doyle replied.

Doyle added to Wright's story by explaining that four men came out of the woods to join Renfroe and shoot at Billings. The horse fell first and Billings was shot as he ran. The rest of Doyle's statement went over previous testimony and irrelevant ground. Compounding the confusion, Doyle singled out the Hillman present in the courtroom as the William Hillman for whom he had worked. Since by then even the prosecution admitted the prisoner was Philip A. Hillman, doubt was cast on all of Doyle's statements. Defense attorney R. H. Smith listed so many inconsistencies in the Negro's remarks that lawyer W. W. D. Turner pleaded Doyle as an ignorant witness.[5] Unconvinced, a Republican paper commented, "No testimony could be strong enough to convict in the minds of some of the sympathizers and apologizers for these 'gentlemanly' murderers." [6]

At 3:30 P.M. Commissioner Gillette adjourned the hearing until five o'clock. At that time the examination continued for the prisoners who were described by the New Orleans *Picayune* as "quiet, respectable looking young men. . . ." [7]

Alfred Wright, father of Richard and the man who had signed the affidavit leading to the arrests, took the stand. He knew Renfroe and Bullock but not Hillman. Renfroe was acclaimed for his marksmanship, especially with the popular Colt's Navy Six. Wright had once seen Renfroe aim his Navy Six and kill a hound dog at two hundred yards. Although Wright was no doubt exaggerating, the exhibition of accuracy caused the Negro to give Renfroe a wide berth thereafter.

Wright was at the Parker place when Billings made his speech; it was a partisan Republican oration but not an abusive one. Wright did not see any of the prisoners at the Parker place. The relationship between Billings and Wright had been close: "I was a kind of scout for Billings, to find out what the white folks were saying about him, and keep him from harm, as I considered him a fair man who wanted to do what was right."

Billings had not planned to go home until Tuesday, August 4. He changed his mind when Bob Ashford—a key witness who could not be located by either side—approached him after the speech. Wright, who was sitting nearby, said Ashford informed Billings in a normal conversational tone that Mrs. Billings was ill and wanted him to come home. Billings used Wright's horse (the animal was actually owned by the Negro's employer).

[5] Mobile *Register*, October 7, 1874; see also New York *Times*, October 7, 9, 1874; New Orleans *Daily Picayune*, October 8, 9, 1874; *Affairs in Alabama*, Nelson Doyle, 548-553; William Taylor (Negro), 745. Apparently Taylor wrote Congressman Hays about Doyle's being a witness to the crime.

[6] Montgomery *Alabama State Journal*, October 8, 1874.

[7] October 9, 1874.

On the Sunday morning following the shooting, Wright met Renfroe, Bullock, and a party of men on a road about two miles from Livingston. Renfroe said, "Here is the man who loaned that damned rascal the horse," but Wright quickly protested that he rented the horse to Billings. "If I thought you loaned him I would kill you," Renfroe answered. At that time Wright did not know a murder had been committed. The band of men let Wright go without harm.

For several days Wright did not see his son, but when he ultimately located him at Meridian and heard the details of the crime, he went to Montgomery. There the Negro hoped to raise enough money to pay the widow Branch for her horse. The Republican state convention was in progress at the capital. After locating Charles Hays and Charles Mayer, a leading Radical politician, Wright related the entire affair. This was the first disclosure the Negro had made to anyone. Hays said he would take care of the matter at a later time.

Wright remembered previous occasions when he had over-heard Renfroe and others discussing Billings at Tartt's store in Livingston. These conversations, in general, had condemned Billings as a trouble maker, a man who attempted to stop the Negroes from working. Renfroe had done most of the talking. The witness contended he had kept quiet because to do otherwise would have meant reprisal. That the danger was real could be seen in the actions of Billings' partner Greata who "got out of his Livingston office like rain."

Since Wright had not been a witness to the crime, his testimony had been designed to reveal a conspiracy. John Little Smith, attorney for the defense, maintained there was not a scrap of evidence proving a conspiracy. Although Wright could not be shaken, the district attorney was forced to admit that he had written the affidavit which the Negro had signed.

The prosecution closed with the testimony of the Negro John Tolliver, although his usefulness as a witness was dubious. Tolliver had met Billings at different times and heard him speak. He knew Renfroe and Bullock but had never heard either discuss Billings. For that matter, he had never heard Renfroe threaten anybody (as a Mobile paper reported it) "but John, and dat's me." [8]

In addition to bringing out the facts relating to the crime, the government attorneys had the witnesses comment on the harmful effects the murder had on Republican chances for political success in Sumter County.

The first witness for Renfroe was Harvey Williamson, a thirty-year-old white man who lived five miles from the defendant. A constable, Williamson passed Renfroe's house on the day of the murder about two hours before sunset and saw the accused pulling fodder in his cornfield. Williamson was on his way to make an arrest, but failed and, returning, passed Renfroe's house once again. It was a half hour before dark, and this time Williamson stopped for a drink of water which the shirt-sleeved Renfroe gladly supplied. They talked briefly about the condition of Renfroe's fodder. Since Renfroe lived at least eight miles from Billings, it would have been impossible for him to be at the site of the crime when it occurred.

William Ormond, a neighbor who lived a mile from Renfroe on an adjoining farm, testified he saw Renfroe at home on the fateful Saturday when the sun was "say three-quarters of an hour high." Ormond, a Baptist, had gone to borrow Renfroe's buggy to take his sister to church on Sunday. Renfroe, he said, was sitting in the doorway of his tenant, Old Pete, watching him make baskets. Other Negroes were also present. Ormond went home just before dark.

A Negro tenant farmer named William Cliff, who had lived with Renfroe for two years, swore that he and three Negroes helped Renfroe take in fodder on August 1. Cliff came to Mobile with William Ormond because "I was told Mr. Renfroe was to be tried, and I got a note telling me to come to Mobile."

---

[8] Mobile *Register*, October 7, 1874; see also New Orleans *Picayune*, October 8, 1874. *Affairs in Alabama*, John Tolliver, 894, had heard Bob Ashford deliver the message to Billings; Alfred Wright, 559, was asked months later if Renfroe and others had long been terrors in the community. He answered, "Lord have mercy upon us! Yes, sir; ever since the surrender."

The statements of young Richard Wright were disputed by James M. Winston, who lived two miles from Ramsey's Station. Winston discussed the topography of the land and the sequence of events. His remarks made Wright's story of how he got to Billings' place seem doubtful. In addition, Winston said there was no dinner at Ramsey's Station on the day in question (there was a Grange dinner there several days after Billings was killed).

The last witness for Renfroe was another Negro tenant, Henry Davis. He retold the forage gathering story of William Cliff and remarked that he saw Renfroe feeding his stock at "good dark."

The next witnesses appeared in behalf of Bullock. Edward B. Tartt explained that Bullock lived in his house and farmed with him on land located eight or ten miles from Billings' place. On the day of the murder Bullock worked on the farm. Tartt saw him feeding his mules between sundown and dark. Tartt elaborated: he had been with Bullock after supper, they talked and later went to bed.

Bullock's brother, N. B. Bullock, who lived three miles from Bullock and Tartt, was sworn and recounted seeing the accused at four o'clock in the afternoon on August 1. Still another witness was John Tartt who confirmed the presence of both Bullocks at Ed Tartt's place on Saturday. John Tartt could not be moved by cross-examination from his story that Charles Bullock remained at home until after supper.[9]

This ended the hearing for the first day, Tuesday. The New York *Times* reported the testimony of the prosecution's witnesses "was incoherent, and they contradicted themselves frequently."[10] Despite such statements, the defense was concerned about countering the remarks made by Alfred Wright. The lawyers moved the court to adjourn the case until they could secure another witness. The district attorney objected, and the court ordered the case to proceed at its scheduled time, Wednesday at 11 o'clock.

[9] Mobile *Register*, October 7, 1874.
[10] October 9, 1974.

When the hearing resumed all of the testimony concerned Hillman. Two men, lawyer A. W. Cockrell of Livingston and grocery owner Thomas W. Sims of Mobile, positively identified the man in the court as Philip A. Hillman, not William Hillman. The hearing ended on this note. Unless it could be proved that the witnesses for the defendants had perjured themselves, they had provided the accused with strong alibis.[11]

Commissioner Gillette announced his decision at 2:30 that afternoon. He mentioned that he was merely a committing magistrate, not one charged with deciding the constitutionality of the Enforcement Acts, although he personally thought the act applied to just such a case as the Billings murder. Gillette said, "there is probable cause to believe that Stephen Renfroe, Charles Bullock and Hillman were of the party committing the crime." If this statement dimmed any hopes for a dismissal, they were extinguished entirely when the commissioner declaimed, "I have been unable to divest my mind of a strong presumption of the guilt of the prisoners Renfroe and Bullock, raised by the direct and clear evidence of the government witnesses."[12]

Renfroe and Bullock were committed without bail to wait trial before the United States Circuit Court. Hillman was discharged, but was forced to give bond to answer a new charge, that of having whipped Nelson Doyle. Chiles, who was to have been defended against the charge of having murdered Ivey, had his case postponed indefinitely. The prosecution had not been able to secure any material witnesses. James Brown, the Negro who claimed to have seen Ivey killed, did not appear to testify. Between the time of the arrests and the hearing, Brown had gone to Mississippi to cut crossties and was confused about when and how he was supposed to appear at Mobile.[13]

Reaction to Gillette's verdict was immediate. From their cells, Renfroe, Bullock, and Chiles had already issued a plea for white solidarity. They hoped:

---

[11] For a suggestion that the defense witnesses had been paid to perjure themselves see Montgomery *Alabama State Journal*, October 9, 13, 1874.

[12] Montgomery *Alabama State Journal*, October 11, 1874.

[13] *Affairs in Alabama*, James Brown, 508-509.

the white men of Alabama, and especially the young men [will read] of our hardships . . . and unite to a man in ridding our State of the fiends who would humiliate us in every way, handcuff us, put us in irons and chains, and parade us through the country. This can be done by every Democrat in the State voting the Democratic ticket, the white man's ticket, and from our cell we call on you, the white men of Alabama, to unloose the chains of your State by the overthrow of the Radical party in November. We are the victims now, but you may be the next.[14]

The Mobile *Register* reacted to the decision with a lengthy editorial entitled "Incarceration of Innocent Citizens." The paper charged the men had been proved innocent, "But this trial was not the trial of a court of justice. It was the trial of the patience and endurance of the Democratic and Conservative party of Alabama." The prisoners had been "ironed, insulted as the vilest criminals, hauled about like dogs, and treated with ignomity [*sic*] by Deputy Marshals. . . ." The affair had been an "unjust, inhuman and altogether infamous proceeding, which a band of pirates would not dignify with the name of trial. . . ."[15]

At Greenville, the south Alabama town's *Advocate* inferred that the hearing was an insidious political plot. "Let the people think of this," the editor wrote, "and resolve to defend themselves at the ballot box."[16] A man who professed to be a Democrat had better beware, an editor warned, because those "hellhounds are on your track, and as soon as they can succeed in getting someone to swear out a pack of lies against you, your fate will be like that of Renfro and Bullock."[17]

The Montgomery *News* denounced the "cruel, barbarous, insolent, tyrannical proceeding, which calls hereafter for the amplest redress, and for the condign punishment of the actors in the outrage."[18] "If this be not government by scoundrels for the better accomplishment of the designs of scoundrels," the

---

[14] Livingston *Journal,* October 16, 1874, quoting Mobile *Register.*
[15] October 9, 1874; see also Butler *Choctaw Herald,* November 25, 1874.
[16] Greenville *Advocate,* October 8, 1874.
[17] Butler *Choctaw Herald,* October 14, 1874.
[18] Quoted in Mobile *Register,* October 10, 1874.

New York *World* wondered, "what is it?"[19] Democrats were relentless in their assertions of Republican duplicity. "The people of Sumter are as peaceable and law-abiding as any to be found in the State," the Tuscaloosa *Times* declared. "But it has suited the ends of their Radical maligners to traduce and misrepresent them in every possible way. . . . They are patriotic and true men, and that is the reason the Radicals hate and slander them." Another Tuscaloosa paper, equally vehement, declared, "The white skinned man who votes the Radical ticket in November next, . . . votes to put his white neighbor in chains and dungeons." [20]

Republican papers such as the Chicago *Inter Ocean* upheld the decision. "Curtis," that paper's southern correspondent, claimed that although Renfroe "is represented by Alabama Democratic papers as a gentleman of wealth and respectability, [he] is in fact the terror of Sumter County." "Curtis" was amazed that "this political desperado is defended by the most respectable Democratic newspapers of Alabama." [21] As for the people of Sumter County, one Radical editor wrote, "We believe . . . that they are perhaps the most openly vindictive and defiant violators of law in all the commonwealth." [22]

Bombastic polemics and sulphuric tirades by both Democrats and Republicans made objective analysis difficult. Impassioned positions aside, the hearing raised several questions that it did not answer. How had Wright and Doyle managed to walk directly past the assassins waiting in ambush without seeing them or their tethered horses? Surely, Renfroe and his companions must have seen the Negroes, and, if so, why would they proceed with the murder in front of witnesses? There would have been other opportunities later. Granted that Renfroe and his men did not wish to cancel their plans, why would they let the witnesses go

---

[19] Quoted in *ibid.*, October 16, 1874.
[20] Quoted in Montgomery *Alabama State Journal*, October 8, 1874; Tuscaloosa *Blade*, October 15, 1874.
[21] Chicago *Inter Ocean*, October 12, 1874; see *ibid.*, October 9, 1874.
[22] Montgomery *Alabama State Journal*, October 8, 1874; see *ibid.*, October 9, 1874.

free? If Renfroe and Bullock were guilty, they did not set a high level of professional competence in the black art of murder.[23]

Renfroe and Bullock were interviewed in October by "H. C.," a correspondent for the New York *Times*. A federal officer told the journalist Renfroe had killed at least fifty men, and the writer expected to encounter two savage and formidable men. "I was exceedingly surprised to find the prisoners mild-mannered gentlemen who spoke easily and well upon every question of the day. . . . Mr. Bullock is a simple, good-natured man, who looks what he is, a Southern farmer. Renfroe, on the contrary, is possessed of more than ordinary intelligence, and is evidently a man of refined feeling." Both men claimed they were at home when the crime was committed. Renfroe said he had seen Billings once, sometime before the murder, and they had a friendly conversation. Bullock declared he had never seen the deceased before or after the murder. Both spoke calmly and dispassionately. Renfroe made one comment about the testimony: "If I had just killed a man, and had a dozen or more friends at my back, would I not have also killed any chance witness to the deed, instead of offering him $20 to keep silent on the subject?"[24]

The *Times* man had inadvertently selected a poignant moment for his interview. While the reporter was present a keeper came to the cell and handed Renfroe a telegram from his wife. He hastily tore open the envelope, glanced at the dispatch, and, unable to hold back a few tears, exclaimed, "Thank God for that." After a moment Renfroe handed the message to the journalist. It read, "The baby is born safe and well; it is a boy." Later the son was named for his father. Cherry, who was rather delicate, had given Renfroe the only child he would ever have. In words that were both melodramatic and sincere, Renfroe asked his visitor, "Do you think it probable that I would go around the country shooting men who never harmed me, when I was expecting this?"[25]

---

[23] For some other unexplained points see Mobile *Register*, October 11, 1874, quoting Montgomery *Advertiser*.

[24] Mobile *Register*, October 30, 1874, quoting New York *Times*.

[25] *Ibid.*

Taken from any angle, the hearing had indeed been a strange one. While Renfroe and Bullock were still in prison a bewildering series of events ocurred in Sumter County that gave credence to Democratic cries of oppression.

CHAPTER VIII

Vindication

For the time being interest shifted from Renfroe and Bullock to Sumter County. Affairs had reached the stage in Livingston that outsiders were understandably dubious about accounts purporting to describe conditions there. Several Northern and Southern journalists and writers came to Sumter to see for themselves. Reports that armed men were constantly riding about, that Negroes were being intimidated, that life and property were insecure were either grossly exaggerated or entirely untrue one newspaperman wrote.[1] As for Sumter County, "If the half that has been said of her was true," another auditor chronicled, "neither white nor black would remain in her borders." [2] "W" wrote an article designed to correct the impression of whites who breakfasted daily on carpetbagger steaks and served scalawag soup for dinner.[3]

Why all the confusion? Why were events being misunderstood and misinterpreted? "Z. L. W.," correspondent for the New York *Tribune*, came to Livingston for the express purpose of finding out. He stared in disbelief at the unusual panorama of army tents around the courthouse and sentries walking their posts. More in keeping than the roll of drums was a street scene:

[1] Mobile *Register*, October 23, 1874, quoting "Z. L. W." to New York *Tribune*.

[2] "Sumter" to Mobile *Register*, October 20, 1874.

[3] See letter in Mobile *Register*, October 16, 1874.

he saw a mule team hitched to a wagon containing two bales of cotton lightly attended by a Negro boy dozing on top. People went about their affairs, and business survived in incongruous ways: one man sold apple pies to the soldiers for forty cents a dozen. "Z. L. W." saw little evidence of violence.[4]

The various writers did not fully realize that behind the routine of daily existence events were approaching a climax. Federal soldiers and detectives were present; there had been murders and arrests; there was resentment because Renfroe and the others had been jailed; racial tension had increased; and the situation was exacerbated as state and county elections grew closer.

On Friday, September 18, the Patrons of Husbandry, an agricultural organization more commonly known as the Grange, held a barbecue at Livingston. The afternoon festivities were interrupted by a group of muddy horsemen who rode into town and dismounted at the sheriff's office. The men had clearly been riding hard, their mission's urgency explained by a note from Dr. William McPherson of Belmont. The physician-planter, who lived in the county's eastern section near the Tombigbee River, reported a large mob of Negroes drilling and parading on his property. Some of them, he thought, had participated in recent difficulties in Greene County. The Negroes refused to disperse, prompting the doctor to ask the aid of Sheriff Samuel Williamson.

The disquieting news was made doubly so because it followed hard on the heels of an affair that had occurred on September 9 at Preston Beat near Gainesville. A Negro named Warren Dew had frightened many Gainesville citizens into believing he intended to destroy the town by fire. Following the advice of a Republican solicitor at Gainesville, the whites asked the sheriff for aid. He sent his deputy, Robert Williamson (who was also his brother), but the Negroes were unimpressed with his authority, although they denied any intention to cause trouble. Finally, Sheriff Williamson calmed matters down by appearing with a

---

[4] Mobile *Register*, October 21, 1874, quoting "Z. L. W." to New York *Tribune*.

posse and making fourteen arrests. A climate of fear, however, had been created, and the Preston Beat difficulty helped trigger the next crisis: the "Belmont Riot." [5]

At the suggestion of his attorney, William G. Smith, the sheriff responded to Dr. McPherson's request by raising a posse of about forty men. Their departure that night, among other things, caused postponement of a fancy ball planned by the Grangers. Reaching the vicinity of Belmont the next morning, some members of the posse intercepted Negro mailman Thomas D. Long, relaxed and astride a mule, ambling slowing toward Livingston on the mail run from Demopolis. Anticipating possible difficulties, the men warned the Negro to turn back, and, unperturbed, he did so. (It was symptomatic of the times that this would be reported in a Radical paper as the forceable stopping of a mail train and wanton rifling of its contents.)

Frightened white women and children from the surrounding countryside had gathered at Belmont for safety. Sheriff Williamson found armed citizens, a group of volunteers from Mississippi, and a posse from Demopolis. There were stories of Bob Reed as the ringleader, and the whites, by now numbering two hundred men, searched the swamps at nearby Durden's Ferry. No concentration of armed blacks was discovered. In fact, only five Negroes were found. They were arrested, marched to Belmont, and placed under a peace bond. Bob Reed and his family had fled their cabin. When a detachment of Captain Mills' men reached Belmont on September 21, the so-called riot was over. Both whites and Negroes had returned to their farming operations.

Although their fear was genuine, the whites had never been in danger. Negroes from the area gave abundant and convincing testimony that they were neither drilling under arms nor holding clandestine meetings. They admitted attending political conclaves, but without exception insisted on listing Bob Reed's strictures against using any form of violence. Their only weap-

[5] *Affairs in Alabama,* William Overton Winston, 632; Jackson Warmouth (Negro), 760; Warren Dew, 914; Ceasar Davis (Negro), 942-948; Captain William Mills, 1057; Mobile *Register,* October 20, 1874, quoting "Sumter."

ons were those used to shoot game. The absence of Negroes from their homes could be explained in terms of their own fear of being raided. Rumors and realities of white posses or even Ku Kluxers and White Leaguers frightened them and drove them into the swamps.[6]

Fortunately and perhaps surprisingly, no one was injured. No random posse member, emboldened by whiskey—testimony revealed that quantities were consumed—and inflated with his new position, shot anyone. In fact, the posse, despite the wild scramble of horses, buggies, and wagons, maintained excellent discipline. Even when the frustrated men found Reed's empty cabin, the extent of their damage was to free several horses from his corn crib and raid his sweet potato patch.[7]

At Livingston Hester soon assumed the lead in ferreting out criminals and bringing Democrats to heel. Whites saw his maneuvers as deliberately calculated to disgrace Democrats and assure Republican dominance. Appointed a deputy United States marshal by Healy "because I presumed he would be more effective than even my own men," Hester, dressed in a brown homespun suit and girdled by a revolver belt, operated out of a room in Bell's Hotel. A footsquare piece of cardboard was tacked to the door and inscribed with the words "U. S. Marshal's Office." Beach was also made a deputy marshal, but played a minor role because tramping through Sumter County swamps made him ill. He was confined to bed for two weeks and disabled for two more.[8]

---

[6] See *Affairs in Alabama* for testimony of the following blacks: Alexander Bates, 412-417; Tony Taylor, 420; Cyrus Abram, 422-424; Jordan Hill, 424-427; William Taylor (former member of the state legislature), 744; Daniel Mimms, 750; Levi Clemens, 771; James H. Inge, 779; George Chiles, 863; Henry Henderson, 649. Bob Reed was obviously an able man. See testimony of Dr. William B. Jones, a Republican, 649.

[7] For details of the Belmont Riot see *Affairs in Alabama*, Samuel Williamson, 751-753; Addison G. Smith, 865, 868-869; William McPherson, 1178-1184; Caleb J. Landrum, 902-907; Joseph W. Jenkins, 896; William D. Battle (town marshal), 1160-1162; Joseph G. Hester, 1014; Captain William Mills, 1047-1048, 17051, 1057; Tony Taylor (Negro), 418-419.

[8] *Ibid.*, Robert W. Healy, 329; Josiah N. Beach, 1193; Mobile *Register*, October 21, 1874, quoting "Z. L. W." to New York *Tribune*. See also reports for October 31, November 1, 9, 1874, in Roll 171, RG 94, National Archives.

Issuing *ex cathedra* pronouncements and armed with warrants, Hester embarked on a whirlwind routine. He undertook no less a project than arresting all of the men involved in the Belmont riot. In his opinion they had violated the Enforcement Acts by trying to kill Reed and by turning back the mailman. Did this mean arresting an entire posse? It did, and Hester—aided at times by Beach and Randolph—rode about the county with a military escort making arrests.

One afternoon lawyer James Cobbs gazed incredulously from his office window in Bell's Hotel at the sight of forty-two men on horses and mules riding into town in the company of Hester (attired in a military cap and overcoat) and the military. From the vantage point of another window a visitor to Livingston also watched the strange procession. The men dismounted and were paraded in a line on the courthouse green. Hester's sorties into the Belmont area had not been especially productive until he informed certain leading whites they were under arrest. At that, most of those cited voluntarily surrendered and formed the large group that he escorted to the courthouse. Hester said later the men waived hearings and after signing bonds of $100 each was bailed. The preparation of bonds lasted until after nine that night, and the men—tired, bitter, and hungry—mounted their equally disgruntled animals for the long rides to their country homes.[9]

Of all the men arrested, Thomas Cobbs was the only one who got a hearing. Commissioner Wayne released him—because he was innocent, Cobbs claimed; because the Negro mail carrier did not appear to testify, Hester rejoined. At all events, Cobbs was freed but not before his lawyer, Thomas B. Wetmore, and Hester had a bitter argument. A New York reporter believed Hester quit pressing for other hearings because he knew the men would have been freed. It would be better to have no examination until after the election.[10]

[9] "W" to Mobile *Register*, October 16, 1874; *ibid.*, November 1, 1874, quoting "Z. L. W." to New York *Tribune*.

[10] *Affairs in Alabama*, William H. Wayne, 671-672; Joseph G. Hester, 1012-1013, 1031. Fearing the possibility of an altercation, Wayne had been reluctant to hold the hearing. See also Mobile *Register*, November 1, 1874, quoting "Z. L. W." to New York *Tribune*.

Two weeks later Hester struck again. This time he arrested Sheriff Williamson himself and a Negro named Scipio Coleman. Williamson explained later that he understood he was charged with having knowledge of Ivey's murder before and after the fact. He surrendered the jail keys and was locked up. On the same day Coleman was arrested by a group of Negroes and accused of being the flagman who stopped the train carrying lvey. Williamson demanded but was denied a hearing. Within a few days he gave bond, was released, and the case was dropped. Coleman, without a hearing and without being charged, was also released. Coleman said that while in jail he was greatly abused by the soldiers who tried to make him confess and by Hester who struck him with a pistol.

There seemed litte doubt that Williamson had antagonized Hester and the military. For one thing, even Williamson's friends admitted that despite his former membership in a temperance society, the sheriff was fond of strong drink. Personal habits aside, he was not afraid to state his opinions, and at various times made vocal and public his opinion of military occupation. Why were the sheriff and Coleman released so suddenly? It seems probable that the psychological reaction to some of Hester's activities was being felt as far away as Montgomery or even Washington. Citizens of Sumter County, who had been critical of Radical policies, petitioned Governor Lewis for relief against the indiscriminate arrests. Healy informed Hester that all apprehended persons should have speedy hearings and that he should be careful in making arrests.[11]

A visiting reporter from St. Louis claimed that in many instances white citizens had taken refuge in the swamps but not because they were guilty of crimes. It simply was cheaper to live in swamps until after the election than incur the expenses of being defended by counsel before the United States Commis-

---

[11] *Affairs in Alabama,* Robert W. Healy, 1254; Samuel Williamson, 754, 890; Scipio Coleman, 1156-1157; Thomas B. Wetmore, 936; Benjamin F. Herr, 678, 682-683; Joseph G. Hester, 1012; William M. Brooks, 523; "Sumter" to Mobile *Register,* October 20, 1874.

sioner at Mobile. The writer, although exaggerating, declared, "there is a blight upon the land. The politican on the rampage and the dragoon on his raid are the only signs of activity. God help these poor people." [12]

"Z. L. W." echoed these sentiments, declaring that most whites were not home to callers. He charged, in effect, that Hester and others had "declared martial law in Sumter County."[13] If the people looked critically on Hester as their *de facto* ruler, it should be said in his defense that he was completely dedicated to carrying out his assignment.

Captain Mills was ordered to neighboring Greene County in October. On October 11, Captain Miles Moylan, " a dashing Irish dragoon" and an officer with a penchant for losing his rank, arrived with a company of the Seventh Cavalry. Booted and spurred, his command included Lieutenant Charles A. Varnum and forty-five enlisted men. Although the cavalrymen did not mingle with the people, they arrived after most of the arrests and been made and were more popular than Mills' soldiers had been.[14]

A final move was made by Hester on October 18. On that day he arrested lawyer Wetmore. The two had previously clashed, and now Wetmore was charged with conspiring to intimidate Hester in the discharge of his duty. Wetmore was also chairman of the county Democratic Executive Committee and when arrested was on his way to attend a Democratic meeting, the first such gathering since the arrest of Renfroe. Also taken into custody were twenty-year-old Stephen Smith and John Little, the Negro leader who had become an influential and articulate

[12] Mobile *Register*, October 25, 1874; quoting "A. C. B." to St. Louis *Republican.*

[13] Mobile *Register*, November 1, 1874, quoting New York *Tribune.*

[14] *Affairs in Alabama*, Lieutenant Charles A. Varnum, 729; Secretary of War William W. Belknap's letter showing the number of federal troops in Alabama, 1284; Mobile *Register*, October 25, 1874, quoting "A. C. B." to St. Louis *Republican;* "W" to Mobile *Register*, October 16, 1874. Moylan's troops had been stationed at New Orleans. See Returns From U.S. Military Posts 1800-1916, Roll 638 . . . See also reports for September 30, October 9, 1874, in Roll 170, RG 94, National Archives.

Democrat. These three men were taken the next day to Mobile
to face Commissioner Gillette, and once again Democratic papers
remonstrated with angry claims of political persecution.[15] Requests for hearings before one of the United States Commis-
sioners at Livingston were turned down, and it was alleged that
subpoenas for witnesses had been issued two weeks before the
offense was supposed to have been committed.[16] The prisoners
were escorted to Mobile by Hester and other guards and report-
edly received better treatment than Renfroe and his companions.
At their hearing, held in late October, the evidence was so flimsy
that Little was discharged and immediately became a witness
for Wetmore and Smith.

An unusual event intruded into the life of special agent Hester, already under heavy attack by Alabama, North Carolina,
and New York newspapers. Admiral Raphael Semmes, Confederate naval hero who had commanded the famed *Alabama,* lived
at Mobile and was among the spectators at the hearing. The
celebrated Semmes thought he recognized Hester. Yes, he was
sure he remembered the detective. During a break in the proceedings Semmes confronted Hester and reminded him of his
service as Master's Mate on board the Confederate steamer
Sumter which Semmes had commanded in 1861 and 1862. (It
seemed ironic that the ship's name was *Sumter.*) Theirs was
both more and less than a nostalgic reunion of loyal seaman and
beloved superior. Somehow, a story circulated that Hester had
jumped ship at Gibraltar after killing a fellow crewman in a
quarrel. Democratic papers used this incident with unalloyed

[15] Livingston *Journal,* October 23, 1874; Chicago *Inter Ocean,* October
19, 22-23, 1874; Mobile *Register,* October 21, 1874, quoting Meridian
Mercury and New York *World;* and October 22, 1874, quoting Selma
Times and Selma *Echo.* The *Register,* of course, also condemned the
arrests. For various viewpoints of the principals see *Affairs in Alabama,*
Addison G. Smith, 874; Thomas B. Wetmore, 918, 822; Benjamin F. Herr,
681; and Joseph G. Hester, 1013, 1035.

[16] This charge was brought in Chicago *Inter Ocean,* October 24, 1874;
for Hester's affidavit against Wetmore see Mobile *Register,* October 23,
1874. See also *Affairs in Alabama,* William M. Brooks, 514-515, 522-523.
Brooks, a Dallas County politician, was at Livingston to speak on the
day Wetmore was arrested. He said the military and the detectives intimidated the people of Sumter County.

delight. Hester later produced impressive evidence, including a letter from Admiral Semmes, that he had served honorably on board the cruiser *Sumter*.[17]

Gillette's decision was of considerable importance. To release the accused would invalidate Hester's Sumter County exploits and would undoubtedly aid the Democrats in the pending elections. To bind them over for trial would be difficult because no evidence of consequence had been presented. Caught in this dilemma, Gillette adroitly announced he was postponing his decision for two weeks. Democrats observed that by then the November elections would have occurred and seemed to have some reason for charging the delay was based more on the dictates of politics than of justice.[18]

With two weeks to wait, the men returned home where Wetmore and Little campaigned for the Democratic ticket. It did little good. The local and state Republican candidates won lopsided victories. The Radical majority of 1,620 represented an increase of 821 votes over Grant's total in 1872. Sumter Democrats attributed their defeat to military pressure, intimidation of Negroes, importation of voters, and every other means of political fraud.[19] Because the entire county was disrupted and in a state of near political chaos, it is impossible to evaluate or analyze the vote accurately.

Democratic wails of anguish in Sumter were drowned out by exclamations of victory elsewhere in the state. The resurging

[17] See Mobile *Register*, October 24, 1874, quoting New Work *World;* and the issue of October 29, 1874, quoting New York *Sun* and Wilmington [North Carolina] *Morning Star.* For the Semmes-Hester confrontation see Mobile *Register*, October 24, 1874; Chicago *Inter Ocean*, October 24, 1874; *Affairs in Alabama*, Joseph G. Hester, 1019-1020. See also Raphael Semmes, *Service Afloat; Or, The Remarkable Career of the Confederate Cruisers Sumter and Alabama* . . . (New York, 1869), 344-345. For a strong case against Hester see Charles Grayson Summersell, *The Cruise of C.S.S. Sumter* (Tuscaloosa, 1965), 167-171.

[18] For hearing proceedings and comments see Mobile *Register*, October 24-25, 1874; Livnigston *Journal*, November 6, 13, 1874; Chicago *Inter Ocean*, October 24, 1874.

[19] Mobile *Register*, October 31, November 6, 10, 1874. In *Affairs in Alabama*, William Overton Winston, 633, said he saw Mississippi blacks at the polls in Gainesville.

Democrats had in fact elected their state ticket, and, as it turned out, crushed Radical power. Although the complexities of Reconstruction are difficult to follow, the Democrats had succeeded by turning to George Smith Houston, a North Alabama Unionist, and issuing a platform calling for economy in government and white supremacy. They blamed the state's economic stagnation on the Republicans and made it plain that one was either a Radical or a Democrat. The Republicans renominated David P. Lewis, also of North Alabama but a former Confederate leader. In general, the Republicans called for civil and political equality. It might have been confusing for the Democrats to have a Unionist candidate and the Republicans a former Confederate, but the Democrats campaigned vigorously and won.[20]

No city enjoyed election revels more than Mobile (and, in fact, the port city would later be investigated for alleged election irregularities). The state militia that had done patrol duty on election day at the polling places assembled at the jail and serenaded Renfroe and Bullock.[21] With the state "redeemed" and the Sumter County situation the exception rather than the rule, events took a decided Democratic turn. Smith and Wetmore returned to Mobile to face Commissioner Gillette. On November 10, the case was reopened only to be immediately dropped, and the men were discharged.[22] According to one story Smith later obtained satisfaction in a fist fight with Randolph on the streets of Montgomery.[23]

The election victory serenade had shown Renfroe and Bullock they were not forgotten. They became the center of attention once more as their case came up for hearing on a writ of *habeas corpus*. On November 14, United States Circuit Court Judge W. B. Woods agreed that the men could be released and set their bail at $6,000 each. One editor argued that permitting them to post bond so soon after the elections proved the arrests were

[20] See Edward W. Williamson, "The Alabama Election of 1874," *Alabama Review*, XVII (July, 1964), 210-218.

[21] Chicago *Inter Ocean*, November 11, 1874; *Affairs in Alabama*, Emanuel H. Saltiel, 1124.

[22] Mobile *Register*, November 11, 1874.

[23] Herr, "Reconstruction in Sumter County," 16.

political. A friendly newspaper felt sure the money could be raised and $100,000 more in one hour if it were necessary.[24]

The journal did not exaggerate, and on November 15, twelve men signed their bond, although many others also volunteered. Throughout the day scores of Mobilians visited the Sumter County men and offered their congratulations. At ten o'clock that night Renfroe and Bullock were escorted to the depot by a large delegation of citizens. Before the train departed, the men thanked the people of the city for their many kindnesses, causing a reporter to write, "Two more affable, courteous, and genial gentlemen never walked upon our streets, in the full enjoyment of liberty, much less as prisoners." [25]

Bullock returned to Livingston and received a tumultuous homecoming. Renfroe went directly to Meridian, where his wife and son were temporarily residing. There seems little doubt that most people believed both men innocent. A fund-raising reception was given for Renfroe and Bullock at the American Hotel in Gainesville. Renfroe stood up and expressed thanks for the money contributed to help defray their recent expenses but declined to accept. Instead, he requested that the money be donated to the Orphan's Home at Lauderdale, Mississippi.[26] Besides dimming the eyes of the ladies present, this suggestion helped eliminate any lingering doubts about the kind of man he was.

The men had to return to face the Grand Jury in late December, and meantime Renfroe busied himself making arrangements for a place to live. He moved his family to the John Sprott place near Livingston.[27] A local paper reported, "Steve Renfroe is at it again! He has been running three double plows this week, and holding one of them himself. The *State Journal*'s attention is called to this new outrage." [28]

At Livingston the Sumter County Grand Jury turned the tables by indicting the unpopular Hester and Randolph for hav-

[24] Butler *Choctaw Herald*, November 25, 1874.
[25] Mobile *Register*, November 17, 1874; see *ibid.*, November 15, 1874.
[26] Livingston *Journal*, November 20, December 4, 1874.
[27] *Ibid.*, November 27, 1874.
[28] *Ibid.*, December 18, 1874.

ing made malicious and false arrests of certain citizens.[29] But by then both men had left the county.

When Renfroe and Bullock returned to Mobile they were welcomed by local citizens for the holidays. The twenty-four-man Grand Jury (four of them were Negroes) listened to testimony by Hester. Curiously, Bob Ashford, the Negro who had carried the message to Billings that supposedly came from his wife, had been located after the original hearing. He was arrested, placed in the Livingston jail, and then released. His testimony would have been important, but at last report he had gone to Texas. After reviewing the evidence, the Grand Jury failed to find a true bill against either Renfroe or Bullock. They were free men.[30]

"No honest man who heard or read the testimony on their examinations before the commissioner believed them guilty," commented the highly regarded Selma *Southern Argus*. "The men who had them arrested knew they were innocent. The witnesses who testified against them committed self-proved perjury." [31] A final statement by the Montgomery *Advertiser*, although unfair, was not entirely untrue: "Hand cuffs are at a discount now and will not be needed until next election." [32]

[29] *Ibid.*, November 13, 1874. *Affairs in Alabama*, G. B. Randolph, 502. Randolph claimed he was merely trying to arrest Alonzo Kornegay who was supposedly hiding at a neighbor's house.

[30] Mobile *Register*, December 25, 27, 29, 31, 1874; January 14-15, 1875. For the arrest of Ashford on October 11, *after* the hearing, see Livingston *Journal*, October 23, 1874; see *ibid.*, December 18, 1874; January 1, 8, 29, 1875. "Curtis" in Chicago *Inter Ocean*, January 23, 1875, wrote that because a majority on the Grand Jury were Democrats, securing an indictment was impossible; *Affairs in Alabama*, William H. Wayne, 669.

[31] February 5, 1875.

[32] January 5, 1875; for similar sentiments see Livingston *Journal*, January 29, 1875.

CHAPTER IX

Hero–Sheriff

B y 1875 political peace was slowly returning to Alabama. The "Negro problem" was not solved, but white Democrats were in such effective control that racial disturbances were rare, and in general life was assuming a more languid pace. The permanence of the 1874 Democratic victory was proved by the elections of 1876. In August Renfroe joined other Democrats in winning the county and state elections by a majority of 868 votes. The November presidential election was still another Democratic victory. In the county Samuel J. Tilden defeated Rutherford B. Hayes 2,238 to 1,370—a greater majority than Grant had received over Greeley in 1872.[1] The Republican party had been eliminated as a potent political force in the state. Although Hayes was the victor nationally in a disputed election, federal troops were withdrawn from the South. Editor Herr wrote wistfully, "Were it not for an occasional sight of a cavalry jacket on the back of a negro, we would feel like 'refugeeing.' " [2]

In the spring of 1875 Renfroe took time off from farming to make a modest entry into politics; he was elected alternate delegate to a beat meeting. For the most part Renfroe concentrated on farming, and by June 1876 his cotton fields won accolades

---

[1] Livingston *Journal,* August 11, 18, November 10, 1876.
[2] *Ibid.,* December 8, 1876.

from the Livingston *Journal.* In the spring of 1877 Renfroe brought the first cotton bloom into Livingston.[3] But the momentum of Renfroe's past made it difficult for him to accept the unexciting life of a cotton farmer. The danger and excitement of the War and the Reconstruction years were not easily forgotten, and at the very least he was bored. The county was quiet for the first time in many years. The carpetbaggers had departed; the scalawags had capitulated; the soldiers had gone West to fight the Indians. The intrepid Captain Moylan and his men would join George S. Custer and be a part of the command that survived the disaster at Little Big Horn in 1876. First the Ku Klux Klan and then the White League had disbanded. There was no trouble from the Negroes and none was anticipated.

Martial memories were stirred when the old Sumter Rifles were reorganized with S. H. Sprott as captain and Renfroe as first lieutenant. But for the second in command such ersatz military activity was tame at best.[4] Although Renfroe was not yet thirty-five, his exploits were already legend. As much as anyone, he was credited with redeeming the county from Radical control. He was young, respected, and had a fine wife and son. One might not grow wealthy as a cotton planter, but it was a comfortable and fairly certain way to grow old. Yet an anticlimactic life had no appeal for a man like Renfroe.

In April 1878, a *Journal* correspondent commented on a rumor. Was Renfroe planning to run for sheriff? Several other men had already announced for this important post. Speculation ended when Renfroe replied in a letter "I am a candidate, and intend to submit my claims to the Democratic convention, if one be held. I ask all my friends to support me." [5]

On July 6, Dr. D. H. Williams gaveled the Democratic county convention to order. The Gainesville native had come over to the Livingston courthouse expecting to preside over a close contest for sheriff's nomination. Among the nominees were Ren-

[3] *Ibid.,* June 4, 1875; June 19, 1876; June 15, 1877.

[4] *Ibid.,* October 22, 1875.

[5] For Renfroe's letter see *ibid.,* April 27, 1877; see also issues of April 20, June 18, 1877.

froe, D. W. Mitchell, Joseph A. McConnell, and Josephus Wallace. On the first ballot Mitchell led with thirty-two votes, Renfroe was second with twenty-two. After the end of the fifth ballot Mitchell still had thirty-two votes but Renfroe was up to twenty-six and a half. Under convention rules Wallace was dropped (as low man) after the fifth ballot. On the sixth ballot McConnell was eliminated after Mitchell garnered thirty-four votes and Renfroe thirty-four and a half. Renfroe was declared the winner on the seventh ballot when he gained the votes of fifty delegates to Mitchell's forty-eight.[6]

Renfroe conducted a forthright campaign—thanking the people for their support, asking for their help, and, in what was described as a "manly, dignified card," declaring:

> I will endeavor to be faithful to the trust reposed in me—
> *impartial* in all my duties, governing myself in the discharge
> of my official duty by the laws of the land strictly adhering to
> the four cardinal virtues, temperance, fortitude, prudence and
> justice. Should I fail to comply with this promise, I will tender
> my resignation, and leave the office to be filled by the Chief
> Executive of your state.[7]

By the campaign of 1878 there were few white Republicans in Sumter County, although there was spawning an Independent movement that drew the support of whites disgruntled by conservative (or Bourbon) Democratic leadership. Because they had no Republican candidates, Negroes tended to support the Independents. John S. Turner, running as an Independent Democrat, opposed Renfroe in the August general election. Herr's *Journal* supported the regular Democrats and emphasized "with S. S. Renfroe to execute the processes of our courts, and to preserve the public peace, who will fear a faithful, prompt and efficient exercise of the powers and duties belonging to and imposed upon the Sheriff of your county?" [8]

The race was close, but Renfroe defeated Turner by a vote of 1,776 to 1,179. Anxious to take over his duties, Renfroe claimed

[6] *Ibid.*, July 6, 1877.
[7] *Ibid.*, July 13, 1877.
[8] *Ibid.*, July 20, 1877.

the office and was recognized by the solicitor. Incumbent Sheriff
D. W. Mitchell maintained that his tenure continued until November and was supported by the circuit clerk. A similar dispute
in Greene County had been decided in favor of the incumbent,
and when the issue came before Circuit Judge Luther N. Smith
(who by now had overcome his carpetbagger label and was widely respected), he listened patiently as Wetmore argued long and
eloquently for Renfroe but ruled against him.[9]

Once Renfroe achieved office, he appointed R. L. McCormick
as his deputy. An incident occurred shortly that convinced Sumter countians they had made a wise choice in selecting their chief
law enforcement officer.

There had been persistent complaints against train gamblers
or "monte" players operating between Vicksburg and Selma.
Renfroe and Deputy McCormick went to York one Saturday
afternoon in December with papers to make arrests. They
boarded the Meridian bound train and spotted two of their men.
They made the arrests near Cuba, took their prisoners off,
awaited a return train, and brought their men to Livingston.
As Renfroe boarded the return train he saw two other wanted
monte players, but they quickly fled. Renfroe reasoned they
would be on the next train and authorized one P. G. Edmonds
to take them into custody. Aided by another man, Edmonds
made the arrests and notified Renfroe, who returned to bring
them in. The four men were tried the same day. They pleaded
guilty and were fined $20 each.

Renfroe handled the entire business with professional ease.
McCormick refused a $10 bribe by one of the prisoners attempt-
ing to purchase his freedom. Later in the night one of the
prisoners asked the sheriff to accompany him outside the jail.
Renfroe humored the culprit, but they were scarely outside when
the prisoner thrust a pistol in the lawman's face and demanded
that he accompany him as far as the depot. Apparently the gun
had been stolen from one of the guards. The card shark had
selected the wrong man because Renfroe knocked him down,
retrieved the pistol, and casually took the prisoner back to jail.

[9] *Ibid.*, August 10, September 28, October 5, 19, November 2, 1877.

The would be escapee faced an extra charge of assault with a weapon (this only amounted to an additional fine of $10 since Renfroe felt it unnecessary to trouble himself by pressing charges of attempted murder).[10]

There seemed little doubt of it. Renfroe was an efficient sheriff.

---

[10] *Ibid.*, November 16, December 21, 1877; January 4, 1878.

CHAPTER X

The Downfall

D uring his first months as sheriff Renfroe ran his office smoothly and effectively. He gave no outward signs of instability and scrupulously carried out the minutest administrative details required of his position. The sheriff's letter-book—written in Renfroe's controlled and beautifully formed script—recorded the affairs of a busy office. Surviving correspondence between Renfroe and law officials in other parts of the state indicates a thorough knowledge of his position and a prompt execution of its demands.

In April 1878 an event occurred which disturbed the people of Livingston. The sheriff's courthouse office was burglarized and robbed of $600. The bold thief entered through a window, then forced the doors of a cabinet open with a chisel. He obviously knew where the money was kept because none of the desk drawers were opened. Some private papers from the office of the Register in Chancery were also stolen. The more suspicious citizens were not just disturbed; they were outraged. Two men were arrested as suspects but were released for lack of evidence.[1]

Despite the questionable circumstances of the robbery, Renfroe retained the respect and trust of the people. That his credit was good was seen when R. H. Seymour loaned him $172.50, accepting as security the lawman's two horses, a bay and a sorrel.

---

[1] Livingston *Journal*, April 5, 1878.

In May, a visiting editor of the Butler *Choctaw News* wrote an editorial about Livingston. Renfroe's office received special praise: "The offices of the Register and Sheriff are models of neatness, and reflect credit upon those officers and the county." [2] This report renewed the lingering doubters' faith in Renfroe.

About a year later Renfroe tried to buy or lease a plantation owned by a Mrs. M. B. Hill of Greensboro, located some forty miles away in Hale County. The negotiations, begun in June and lasting until September, ended without any agreement. Neither party would accept the price-terms demanded by the other.[3] Securing this property would have involved a long range obligation for Renfroe. Such commitments of his future income hardly indicated that the sheriff foresaw any immediate change in his status.

Embedded in Renfroe's nature, the role of a loving husband and devoted father manifested itself. He wanted a home for his family. When his plans for the plantation failed to materialize, Renfroe sold his farm for $3,000 and began construction of a house in Livingston. He employed D. J. Chandler, a Chattanooga, Tennessee, contractor, to build the modest structure—a small, one-story frame bungalow copied from the home of a friend at Eppes Station. Work began in the late fall of 1879, and Renfroe followed its progress closely. He ordered glass, rubber bumpers, and various fittings from Mobile and other cities. The Renfroe family moved into their new home in the winter of 1880.[4]

As befitted a man of his inclinations, Renfroe was interested in firearms. He purchased weapons and shells locally and also from Parker Brothers of Meriden, Connecticut. In September 1879 he ordered from the New England firm a 10-gauge shotgun weighing 10 pounds. The shotgun had a 34-inch barrel and a pistol grip. Renfroe's requirements were demanding: "I prefer

[2] Sumter County Deeds, Book 2, April 29, 1878, 126. The Butler *Choctaw News* article was quoted in Livingston *Journal.* May 10, 1878.

[3] S. S. Renfroe to Mrs. M. B. Hill, June 13, 1879; S. S. Renfroe to Thos. R. Ronehac [agent for Mrs. Hill], September 29, 1879, Letterbook of S. S. Renfroe; on file at the Sumter County Courthouse.

[4] Sumter County Deeds, Book 11, January 1, 1880, 519; S. S. Renfroe to D. J. Chandler, October 26, 1879, and January 27, 1879, Letterbook of S. S. Renfroe.

a gun that will shoot 'Buck shot' *close* and *accurately* at long range, say 90 or 100 steps, and at the same time capacitated to shoot small shot at snipe, quail, squirrel, & similar small game abounding in our country." Perhaps the brothers Parker were pleased by his closing remark that "While I have three guns of others' make, I am anxious to have one of yours. . . ." The same month he wrote the company inquiring about a gun he was having repaired, and urging its speedy delivery because he was entering a shooting match at Livingston in November. Satisfactory service, he remarked, would induce others in Sumter County to do business with the company.[5]

In March 1880 Renfroe's hunting mare ran away from him, causing the sheriff to take an unheroic (and embarrassing) spill. Worse luck, he broke his gunstock—"universally admired for its beauty of material and symmetry." Renfroe ordered pink edge wads, shells, and caps, and asked Parker Brothers to remake the stock complete with the initials, "S. S. R." engraved on a silver-plated shield.[6] Properly armed and seemingly carrying out his duties, Renfroe appeared the model of a law officer.

During the early part of 1880 a certain confidant evoked from Renfroe an announcement of his intention of running for office again, only this time for tax collecter. Evidently feeling himself master of his situation, he philosophized in a letter to a friend: "I think that a man, to be successful has to *attend strictly* to his business. If he does not he very soon has no business." [7]

During the ensuing months, however, shadows began crisscrossing Renfroe's career as sheriff. In glaring incongruity with former expressions of his sentiments, he began resorting to the old pattern of violence. Renfroe's equivocal activities became the subject of worried discussions among his friends as well as his enemies. What became flagrant misuses of his offices were later listed by Frank Herr, son and future successor of Livingston

---

[5] S. S. Renfroe to Parker Bros., September 6, 18, 1879, Letterbook of S. S. Renfroe.

[6] See *ibid.*, to *ibid.*, March 18, 1880.

[7] S. S. Renfroe to J. B. Williams, January [?], 1880: see also Renfroe's letters to W. B. Gere, February 7, 1880; and Capt. J. H. Holmes, March 11, 1880, *ibid.*

Journal editor, Benjamin Herr: "Renfroe committed robbery, twice, of his own office—drinking, arson, blackmails, thieving and other almost inconceivable outrages." [8]

Addison G. Smith, a lawyer and intimate friend, closely chronicled the specifics of Renfroe's fall. Smith wrote later "It is well established that while he was sheriff he burned the clerk's office, robbed himself of money he had collected for other people, embezzled money, used trust funds, turned prisoners out of jail, committed an unprovoked assault with intent to murder, and was guilty of various thefts."[9]

Whatever the reasons—complex, elemental, and in combination—Renfroe could no longer walk the precarious path between the lawless and the law-abiding. Citizens of Sumter County were faced with the pressing problem of relieving him of his position as sheriff. As chief magistrate, Renfroe participated in the selection of Grand Juries, was responsible for them during their sessions, and was the only officer qualified to execute their decisions. One story credited District Attorney Wirtz Coleman with devising a solution. On the eve of the Grand Jury's adjournment for the Spring term 1880, it was decided to appoint Coroner Parker to act as sheriff. A secret meeting of the Grand Jury returned six or seven indictments against Renfroe, and he was immediately arrested.

This version of Renfroe's fall erred in a few particulars. Apparently the first indictment against him was lost, necessitating the issuing and filing of a new one. This occurred on April 19, and on April 20, Renfroe, as sheriff, presented to the court the venire for the spring session, including his own indictment. The major charge against him was assault with intent to murder. He was also charged with embezzlement, conversion of money as sheriff, and several citations of negligent escape. Renfroe's bail was first set at $500 then reduced to $300.[10]

---

[8] Herr, "Reconstruction Days in Sumter County," 7.

[9] A. G. Smith, July 17, 1886, to Montgomery *Advertiser*.

[10] Herr, "Reconstruction Days in Sumter County," 8. Herr wrote that it was decided to have a bailiff act as sheriff, but evidently Coroner Parker was selected. See Record of Cases, Book R, April 19, 1880, 20, 22, April 24, 1880, 48; on file at the Sumter County Courthouse.

All the charges against the sheriff were extremely damaging. Yet the loyalty of his friends was ably demonstrated at this point, for in spite of overwhelming evidence of foul play, Renfroe persuaded them to raise money for his release. By May he walked the streets of Livingston, temporarily a free man. Renfroe's plight was dramatized a few days later when the Democrats met in convention to select their slate of county officers. D. W. Mitchell, who had opposed Renfroe in 1878, was nominated for sheriff. Perhaps this act, the formal naming of another man to hold his job, caused Renfroe to lose all restraint. Losing his air of self-possession, Renfroe began drinking, starting fights, and people who had silently applauded the impunity with which he had defied Reconstruction authorities watched with horror the breakdown of a hero. Seeing no way out, several of his sureties withdrew from his Appearance Bond, and early in June Renfroe was re-arrested and committed to jail.

The deposed lawman did not remain in jail long the second time. At 9:30 on Saturday night, June 19, 1880, Renfroe executed his first escape.

Six other prisoners went with him, and although the flight was discovered a few minutes later, no pursuit was organized until one o'clock the next day. Two prisoners, a white woman charged with adultery and Ben Perkins, a Negro awaiting trial for murder, refused to escape (unfortunately for the Negro his belated respect for law went unrewarded as he was later hanged). The Livingston *Journal* reported that Perkins, who was responsible for locking the prisoners in at night, had done his job because all the cell doors were secured. Somehow Renfroe had cut a hole of 15 x 20 inches through the outside wall of his second story cell, led the others through it to a shed roof, and from there to the ground. According to the *Journal*, Renfroe delayed his departure long enough to write a "very piquant note" to Coroner Parker.[11]

While it was patently impossible for Renfroe to have released the other prisoners without a set of keys, it was later claimed that he had anticipated his own arrest and had duplicate keys

[11] June 25, 1880; see *ibid.*, May 7, 21, June 11, 1880.

for the jail and all county offices. Addison G. Smith, not only the sheriff's lawyer but one of the few men whom he trusted, contacted Renfroe a few days later and heard Renfroe explain how he managed the successful flight. When arrested, Renfroe retained a small pocketknife in his shoe. He was permitted an old case knife with which to eat and used his pocketknife to hack the case knife's edge into a crude saw. When Renfroe was allowed out of his cell during the day, he greased the saw so that it made no noise and worked on the jail wall a few minutes at a time. Then he took some of the lime kept in the jail for disinfecting purposes, wet it, and filled in the sawed place so that it appeared to be part of the wall.

When he had completed the task, Renfroe said he persuaded Ben Perkins that as trusty he should steal the cell door key. On the appointed night Perkins opened the cell and released him, after which Renfroe bound the Negro hand and foot, making it possible for the trusty to fabricate a convincing story about outsiders rescuing Renfroe. The ingenious sheriff even had a double-barreled shotgun, possibly the one from Parker Brothers. When confined he had requested the courtesy of a mattress for his cell bunk. The jailor was not aware that the rolled mattress brought into the cell by a Negro boy contained the shotgun.[12]

Because the sheriff's election would not be held until August (when the unopposed Mitchell went into office with 1,680 votes), various people speculated about the legality of the coroner's serving as sheriff for over a month. Aside from the legal complications, Southern decorum required a resignation from Renfroe. Having added escape to the other indictments against him, Renfroe had surely forfeited all claim to office. Yet the Southern code of honor and fair play, in this case illogical but also compelling and admirable, demanded that Renfroe voluntarily step down. If he were still in the county, as many people believed, then lawyer Smith might be able to find him. The involuntarily commissioned attorney agreed to try to locate the fugitive. After making several discreet inquiries, Smith learned that Renfroe

[12] Herr, "Reconstruction Days in Sumter County," 8; A. G. Smith, July 17, 1886, to Montgomery *Advertiser.*

was hiding out in his favorite haunt, the Flat Woods. Smith made his way carefully through the heavily timbered belt along the Mississippi border. He found Renfroe one morning just at daybreak. Seemingly alert even asleep, Renfroe was dozing on a blanket with a double-barreled shotgun at his side. Renfroe seemed reconciled to his new role, described his escape, and willingly signed a statement of resignation. With exacting compliance to the law, Smith or someone forwarded Renfroe's note to the governor, and a paper reported, "How, or from where it was transmitted, we know not." [13]

With Renfroe at large, the fall term of the Grand Jury continued the cases against him. Although his disgrace was total, Renfroe tried to help his family. On July 19, 1880, he signed over his home and property in Livingston to his wife. The statement, witnessed by Smith and E. S. Sledge, made clear that it was in payment for $600 he had borrowed from Cherry in 1873. Even though Cherry had repudiated Renfroe, his legal gesture (doubtless signing over the title had to be arranged at some secret rendezvous) was a decent one.[14]

From late summer 1880 and throughout 1881 no news was heard from Renfroe. People thought his friends kept in touch, but no one in Sumter County reported seeing him. Supposedly he had joined forces with the feared Harrison gang, a group of desperadoes lead by brothers Ben and Robert who operated in Louisiana and Mississippi. In 1881 the indictments against Renfroe had been continued by the Spring Term of the Grand Jury. When it seemed that he had left Sumter County permanently, the August 1881 term of the Grand Jury withdrew most of the indictments, filing them away to be reinstated "as the demands of justice may require." [15]

In June 1882 a New Orleans *Picayune* correspondent reported from Summit, Mississippi (a small town in Pike County which

[13] Livingston *Journal*, July 23, 1880; see also *ibid.*, August 13, 1880; A. B. Smith, July 17, 1886, to Montgomery *Advertiser*.

[14] See Sumter County Deeds, Book 10, July 19, 1880, 558. See also Record of Cases, Book R, October 25, 1880, 87; October 26, 1880, 93-94; October 29, 1880, 102; and Book U, Fall Term, 1880, 146-147.

[15] See Record of Cases, Book R, April 11, 1881, 154; August 16, 1881, 213; Book U, August Term, 1881, 176-178.

borders Louisiana) that fifteen members of the Harrison gang
were encamped near-by. The writer linked Renfroe with the
outlaws, claiming that the band had attempted to rob a store to
secure food. Apparently town authorities had been informed,
and at any event, the holdup failed. The robbery's lack of success thwarted the next part of the plan which had been to rob a
train and escape. The reporter accorded the former lawman
from Sumter County an inflated list of victims: "Renfroe, one
of the gang, supposed to have been seriously wounded, it is
thought is secreted in the woods, if not dead. He is a desperate
man, and has killed his twenty-seven and is wanted every-
where." [16]

As a posse searched the countryside, Mrs. John Harrison confessed that Renfroe, using Smith as his alias, had ridden with
her outlaw sons but had been killed and buried. The whereabouts
of his grave was not revealed. The journalist from the *Picayune*
promised that the "search will be continued and special diligence
will be exerted to recover the body of Renfroe, the escaped
murderer and defaulting sheriff, for whom heavy rewards
have been offered." [17] Placing scant credence in these stories,
the Livingston *Journal* was convinced Renfroe was involved in
the robbery, "But, that he was killed, as stated, we do not believe, and we base this belief on information outside of any
furnished by press reports." [18]

Throughout 1883, with eight indictments lying dormant on
the record books, Renfroe's name, for the first time since the
1860's, did not appear in the Livingston paper. Yet there seems
little doubt that he had returned to Sumter County late in 1882
and was there early in January 1883. A Tuscaloosa newspaper
was scandalized by a private letter its editor had received indicating that Renfroe had gone to Texas after his escape but had
now returned to Livingston. Apparently he arrived at seven one
morning on the Alabama Great Southern Railroad, slipping un-

[16] New Orleans *Daily Picayune*, June 24, 1882.
[17] *Ibid.*, June 25, 1882.
[18] July 7, 1882.

obstrusively off a car at the water tank one mile west of town. Unrecognized, Renfroe walked over to the cemetery (located within the city limits), where he encountered an acquaintance— either by prearrangement or accident. Whatever the case, Renfroe sent the unidentified party to get the city marshal. The compliant law officer met with the fugitive, and the two engaged in a lengthy conversation. The broad daylight parley ended with the marshal's escorting Renfroe to his wife's home. What Cherry and Renfroe said is unknown, but it seems likely that he inquired about his son and asked her to have faith in him.

In Livingston news of Renfroe's presence spread swiftly, causing a worried mayor to warn the city marshal to stay alert. Conceivably the mayor re-evaluated the marshal's qualifications when the lawman revealed that he and Renfroe had spent several hours together. Responding to criticism, the marshal justified his actions with the logic that since Renfroe had returned, it was not unreasonable that he be permitted at least to talk with his wife. Also, Renfroe's ability to maneuver situations to suit his own needs allowed him little difficulty in convincing the marshal that he planned to surrender.

The Tuscaloosa journal commented positively that Cherry "declined to recognize him as her husband." The editor was furious about the turn of events taking place in Livingston. He underlined the untenable situation with the following allegations: Renfroe, angered by his wife's refusal to stick by him, remained in the county and was allegedly entertained by various friends. People not falling into the category of friends were supposedly terrorized or blackmailed. Neither the marshal nor sheriff made any attempt to arrest him, indicating that the "officers of the law are powerless or nerveless." Moreover, the "Negroes are at his beck and call." So sounded the indignation of a mystified and outraged editor.[19]

Whatever the case, Renfroe was by no means forgotten, and he still had friends.

[19] Record of Cases, Book R, Fall Term, 1883, 25-26; Tuscaloosa *Gazette*, January 4, 1883.

Undoubtedly a longing for his wife was not the least of the reasons that compelled Renfroe to risk his freedom in returning home. One of Livingston's residents, Miss Temple Scruggs, then a young girl, recalled hearing her parents discussing Steve and Cherry. Cherry's real feeling of love for Renfroe may have been submerged beneath her feelings of fear. When he visited her in the home they had once shared together, Cherry's brother would walk around the house with a gun. Such vigilance for her safety was hardly conducive to a renewal of former love.[20]

Some of the details of life as a fugitive were supplied by Renfroe himself. In an 1885 interview he told Frank Herr, "Well, Frank, whiskey has so ruined me that I hardly know what I'm doing. I am hardly responsible for anything. It has almost crazed me. When I left here . . . I tried to do right. I struck a number of good jobs and just as I would get to doing well along would come some man and say, 'that's Steve Renfroe; he used to be Sheriff of Sumter Co.,' and that would almost kill me, and I would go to drinking, and that's what ruined me. I haven't been any account since I left here, just because of that." [21]

Excessive indulgence of alcohol was more an effect than a cause of Renfroe's anguish and not the real explanation for the acts of a tormented man. After the confrontation with Cherry, Renfroe left Alabama once again, this time for a year, but Sumter County and the life he had known there formed a psychological magnet to draw him back. Perhaps there was still time to redeem himself. Once more, if all went well, he could command the respect of his neighbors. Salvation lay in returning, surrendering to the law, and accepting whatever punishment awaited him. In the spring of 1884 he returned to Livingston and gave himself up—convinced that this was the first essential step in the long way back.

[20] Authors' interview June 1964, with Mrs. Temple Ennis of Livingston.
[21] Herr Interview, Livingston *Journal*, July 2, 1885.

CHAPTER XI

The Web

No sooner had Renfroe reutrned than his former admirers rallied to his support. They raised his bond, hoping, if not convinced, their imponderable friend would conduct himself properly while awaiting trial. Again his avowals, determined and resolute when made, failed to sustain him in facing the people of Livingston. All desire for regeneration seemed lost when Renfroe began abusing his freedom with his usual antics of getting roaring drunk and fighting. His bondsmen surrendered him to the sheriff, limiting his freedom to that of a cell until the Spring Term of the Circuit Court met.

Renfroe's self-deception was over. He had returned expecting to face his accusers, then either be freed or given a brief sentence. Whether convicted or released, if he endured the ordeal with dignity, his image in Sumter County would have been restored—at least in part. Now it never could be, and his impulsive actions had at last branded him as incorrigible. If Renfroe did not actually spell out his new and final status, he sensed it. No need now to be tried and serve a sentence. His incarceration would stir no emotions except those of relief over his riddance. There was little choice for him—it seemed preferable to be a tarnished fugitive than a former hero wasting away in jail.

It is not difficult to picture Renfroe pacing back and forth from one end of his cell to the other, again and again. Sumter County law officials, well aware of their jail's incredible record of escapes, debated in March 1884 whether to remove Renfroe to the jail at Tuscaloosa, sixty-nine miles away. In April their decision was forced when Renfroe made an escape attempt that almost succeeded.

A small Negro girl was permitted to sleep in the hall of the prison. She, like everyone else in Sumter County, had heard of Steve Renfroe, and he had little difficulty in persuading her to help him. One spring evening she applied a horseshoe nail to his cell door, made some experimental turns, and with great dexterity managed to open it. Renfroe entered the corridor and, forcing the door of another cell, freed one inmate. The two men broke the lock on the outer door at the head of a staircase, but the sounds of their exertions were heard by one Esau, a black who lived in a cabin near the jail. Esau hurriedly sent his daughter for help, clutched an ax, and raced to the jail door. By this time the two fugitives had descended the stairs. They managed to force open the outside door only to be confronted by Esau who held his ax aloft and kept them at bay. Help arrived before they could concoct a plan of rushing Esau, and the escapees were captured and returned to their cells. The attempted flight had failed, but it was obvious that Renfroe could not be held in Livingston. Early in April the closely guarded prisoner was transferred to Tuscaloosa—the entourage gathered a crowd at Eutaw when it passed through. The sturdy Tuscaloosa jail was considered safe, even from the assaults of such a man as Renfroe.[1]

Renfroe's Tuscaloosa cell did not lack for accommodations. There was, among other comforts, a bathtub which sat against the wall. Perhaps Renfroe was merely testing the security arrangements when he made an abortive attempt to escape. Certainly the effort lacked his usual imagination and finesse. The jail's most famous inmate was detected in his cell boring assiduously away at the wall with an auger, an instrument that had been supplied by a Negro woman. He had thrown her a

---

[1] Eutaw *Whig and Observer*, January 31, April 17, 1884. These notes were kindly furnished by the Rev. Franklin S. Moseley of Eutaw, Alabama; see also Butler *Choctaw Herald*, April 17, 1884, quoting Birmingham *Chronicle*.

five-dollar gold piece from his cell window with the request that
she purchase him the auger and keep the change. Somehow she
managed to get the auger inside, but it was unceremoniously
confiscated by the jailor. Undaunted, Renfroe waited for another opportunity.

This soon came in the person of a patent medicine doctor who
was briefly interred in the same cell. In the bottom of a basket
of provisions which the doctor received were a case knife and
fork that escaped the jailor's detection. Renfroe secured this
knife, and, employing a pocketknife that he had smuggled into
the jail, made another saw. He next put the bathtub to an un-
intended use. By sawing through two pipes, one that let out of
the wall and another that drained away water, Renfroe was able
to move the tub. At night he slid it to one side and worked with
his saw on the floor. After cutting a hole about fourteen inches
square, he discovered that the floor was laid on heavy timber,
sixteen inches through. Having a cell on the second floor im-
proved the view but vastly complicated escape attempts. Moreover, the logs were laid against each other so that he could saw
no further. Renfroe decided to burn his way out, but this raised
the problem of obtaining inflammable material.

For the next few days Renfroe became a devoted newspaper
reader. After finishing a paper, he carefully preserved it. As a
nonsmoker, Renfroe had no matches and no way to obtain any.
He quickly acquired the nicotine habit. His matches were supplied by the jailor who gave him one match at a time and stood
at the cell door to watch him light it and see it go out. One day
as the jailor waited for Renfroe to light up, a prisoner in a
neighboring cell called. The jailor departed to see what the
prisoner wanted, giving Renfroe a chance hurriedly to split the
match with his pocketknife. When the jailor returned Renfroe
lit one-half of the match, retaining the other half. The next day
Renfroe was able to light the half match he had and keep the
whole one. This he split, and every time a match was given him
he kept it and lit a half one. When Renfroe had secured thirty-
four matches, he gathered his newspapers and began burning.

At night he put his blanket over the cell door, removed the

bathtub, and set fire to the paper. During his first attempt, Renfroe inadvertently permitted the flames to rise violently to the ceiling, but luckily he doused the fire and afterwards packed wet paper around the cracks to keep the flames from spreading. Renfroe was able to char the logs, rake the charred part out, and put it in the tub. He then replaced the tub and washed the charcoal out through the waste pipe.

By early July he had a hole big enough to slip through but two bulldogs kept in the jailyard posed a final obstacle. On the night of July 7 (July 4 would have suited the occasion better, but he timed his burning improperly), he saved his dinner, waited for the right moment, pushed through the plastering, and swung down into the room below. Renfroe paused long enough to write a good-bye note to the sheriff, adding that he was taking the next train whether it was going North or South. He then lifted a window and stepped into the jailyard. Throwing the dinner which he had saved to the bulldogs, he walked safely by them while they devoured the food. He climbed the outer fence and was gone.

Finding no train convenient, hungry and without money Renfroe made his way to the Black Warrior River. It was morning as he approached the river at a ferry where he persuaded the ferryman to take him across free of charge. On the other side he followed a road until he came to a house. His knock was answered by a woman. Renfroe identified himself as a sewing machine repairman looking for work. It seems doubtful that she believed him, but Renfroe later claimed he repaired her machine, although he had never worked on one before, and the only tool he used was a screw driver furnished by the mistress of the house. He was paid for his efforts with dinner and a half dollar.

Renfroe had pulled off an escape both dramatic and brilliant. Disgruntled newspapers grudgingly praised his feat while reporting that he was free again.[2]

[2] A. G. Smith, July 17, 1886, to Montgomery *Advertiser;* Tuscaloosa *Gazette*, July 10, 1884; Livingston *Journal*, July 11, 1884, wondered "how such a hole could be burned without the smoke or smell of the burning attracting attention?"

After Renfroe left Tuscaloosa, he went to Sumter County but did not remain long. Making his way to New Orleans, Renfroe secured a job working on the "Exposition Building" for a regional fair. He said later he "Passed through Texas, [and spent time] in Mexico working on a bridge force of the Mexican Central Railroad." Then in the early summer of 1885 he decided to return to Sumter County to see his son. Apparently he had given up all hope of effecting a reconciliation with Cherry. "I got as far as Hickory, [Mississippi], on the V[icksburg] & M[emphis] Road, changed my mind and started to Central America, having learned that free transportation would be given to railroad workers in that country. My idea was to go where I would never be known again, and lead a respectable life in some peace." [3]

Renfroe, unable to break away, delayed his departure. For weeks there had been rumors that Renfroe had been seen in the vicinity of Livingston. The reports seem confirmed when on the night of June 17, James Little had a stylish bay horse stolen from his stable. The same evening the thief pilfered a saddle and bridle from William Wessenberg. The thefts were so skillfully managed, it was impossible the next morning to find the direction in which the horse was taken. A Montgomery paper reported, "Suspicion at once fell on ex-Sheriff S. S. Renfroe, whose desperate deeds for nearly two decades, and whose repeated threats have made him the terror of this region." [4]

An angry Little sent a telegram to a Birmingham detective named Sullivan. After reading a description of the horse and the circumstances of the theft, Sullivan considered the terms offered for his services and accepted the assignment. He came to Sumter County, obtained a picture of Renfroe, apparently found some clues, and disappeared. Sullivan was next heard from a week later when Little received a telegram from Slidell, Louisiana, a town located at the eastern end of Lake Pontchartrain and directly across from New Orleans. Terse but triumphant,

---

[3] Interview of Frank Herr with Renfroe in Livingston *Journal*, July 2, 1885.

[4] Montgomery *Advertiser*, July 3, 1885.

the telegram read: "I have the horse. Come down." Little departed for Slidell and on arriving found his horse and, perhaps not unexpectedly, Renfroe.

Sullivan related an intricate tale of pursuit. His quest had taken him to Mississippi where leads, both false and accurate, were found in such towns as Paulding, Heidelberg, and Ellisville (one futile effort took him as far west as McComb). Traveling by horse, foot, and rail, Sullivan finally discovered the thief was making his way down the New Orleans and Northeast Railroad. Incredibly enough, the fugitive seemed to stop at every station. Sullivan boarded a train at Tuscamola, Mississippi, and started South, inquiring at stations along the way.

At Slidell, Sullivan found a Charles Monroe who had purchased the horse from a man named O'Brien. In turn, O'Brien was found and claimed to have sold the animal for a stranger who called himself C. P. Ray. When Sullivan displayed Renfroe's picture, O'Brien identified him as C. P. Ray. Sullivan's informants told him Ray had just gone to New Orleans. Following in close pursuit, Sullivan left instructions to arrest Renfroe if he returned. The detective had scarcely reached New Orleans when he received a telegram reporting Renfroe's arrest at Slidell. Sullivan returned to claim his prisoner. He proved himself a businessman as well as a detective by selling Little's horse, worth an estimated $200, to Monroe for $125—Monroe said he paid $90 originally. The horse was badly used up from riding three hundred miles in one week. Wessenberg's saddle and bridle were also recovered.

Renfroe was taken to New Orleans, where he spared Sullivan and Little the delay of securing a governor's requisition by agreeing to return to Alabama without one. The party reached Livingston at daylight one morning. Renfroe was placed in solitary confinement in the town's new jail—its very construction an unacknowledged memorial to the former sheriff.

Renfroe's version of what occurred (Frank Herr interviewed him in prison and found him "much broken in health and general appearance") was at variance with that of Sullivan. "We found him," wrote Herr, "lying in his hammock, suffering from nausea, and his nervous system completely shattered." Renfroe "spoke very kindly but with great effort." He maintained that he swapped a mule to one J. C. Cook for Little's horse. The exchange took place at Heidelberg. "There was a bill or certificate of the trade in my pocket when arrested, and I suppose it is in possession of the authorities. Cook was on the way to Florida; tried to get me to go with him. If I had stolen the horse I'd hardly have rode him down the railroad track in broad, open daylight, as I did." There was inescapable logic to his words. Either he was innocent or he had deliberately or subconsciously made his own capture inevitable.

Did he live at Slidell? "No, I was on the way to Central America." He had gone to New Orleans and returned to Slidell because "I went to see what it would cost me to have my horse taken across Ponchartrain trestle." Renfroe agreed the animal Cook traded him matched the description of Little's horse and admitted he authorized a man at Slidell to arrange a sale. "He and I were drinking together. He told me he was a good horse trader and knew where he could make a good trade for me. I let him take the horse. When he came back he had a poor old foundered horse and fifteen dollars which he turned over to me."

Was it true he had a pair of Colt's revolvers and saddle bags when he went to New Orleans? "I have not had a pistol since I surrendered to the authorities of this place, more than a year ago. When I went to New Orleans I left a pair of saddle-bags at Slidell. When I returned I was under the influence of whiskey. When I awoke I was under arrest [faced by six captors armed with shotguns, he offered no resistance], my saddle-bags gone and $80 in money taken from my person. I have not seen either since." Herr had heard the stories of Renfroe's presence in Sumter County shortly before his capture, but the prisoner denied being there. He agreed to say more later but complained of being tired. "He is completely broken in spirit and health, the hard life he has led telling on him severely," Herr concluded.[5]

[5] Interview of Frank Herr with Renfroe in Livingston *Journal*, July 2, 1885; A. G. Smith, July 17, 1886, to Montgomery *Advertiser*.

A Montgomery reporter who agreed "his health is broken," speculated, "his career is well-nigh spent. . . ." Yet Renfroe was still impressive physically—his hair and beard were still black and his steel grey eyes still made an impression.[6]

Renfroe's capture and return to Sumter County stirred memories of his past. "The time has been," a journalist recalled, "that he was almost a hero. He was among the first to beard the Republican lion in the Black Belt and he was a leader in the violent times that followed the war." Renfroe was credited with helping rescue the state, and, in fact, "He was bold, fearless, reckless and dashing, just the man to capture the popular fancy when pistols were common and mobs an hourly menace." [7]

Although greatly debilitated, Renfroe realized the August term of the Circuit Court would soon convene. If he were to escape it would have to be quick. It is possible that he still dreamed of going to Central America, and no doubt he wanted the personal satisfaction of escaping from the new jail. Somehow, he got a note to a former friend, J. C. Giles, instructing him to go to Meridian and secure four ounces of nitric muriatic acid and some pure yarn thread. Giles was to dip the string in the acid, then test it on a piece of iron to make sure it would cut metal. If the experiment worked, Giles was to come at night to the rear of the jail, where there was only one window, fasten the bottle of acid and string to the end of a fishing pole, and maneuver them up to his second story cell. The reluctant helper was advised to get aid from a Negro named Dave McGinnis. Renfroe wrote Giles, "It will be no trouble to get out of this place with a little outside help."

Giles declined to accept the role of accomplice. He turned the note over to the sheriff, but the news leaked out and both note and plot were mentioned in the local paper. A special force was detailed to stand guard at Renfroe's cell. Angered by his betrayal, Renfroe wrote a letter to Herr's *Journal* condemning Giles. Although Giles' motives were never made clear, the

[6] Montgomery *Advertiser*, July 3, 1885.
[7] *Ibid.*, July 7, 1885.

prisoner's acerbic reaction was understandable. Accompanying a copy of the original note to Giles was a separate letter to Herr:

> It would perhaps be better for me to say nothing, for I feel that I cannot gain, nor do I expect to get any sympathy from the citizens of this county; but, inasmuch as the JOURNAL has of late made pretty free use of my name, I have concluded to drop you a line in regard to the note written by me to one J. C. Giles.
>
> I did write the note to him. . . .
>
> I am informed that he objected to the note being published because he did not wish the public to know that he had received such a friendly note from me. This is strange, for he has always, when I was AT LARGE, professed the greatest friendship for me. When I have been in the neighborhood he has endeavored to impress upon the community the fact that he knew where I was and could see me whenever he liked. Professing such friendship, I had the right to expect that he would not betray me at least. I find, however, that I was mistaken and that he is a *traitor*. I would not have censured him if he had simply burned the note up and said nothing about it and taken no action in the matter at all. But I suppose he thought that he could safely betray me, now, as I am in Jail, with no hope of escape. Does *any one* believe he would have done it if I had been at LARGE? Why did he not tell the Sheriff where I was when I was in the county—not in Jail?
>
> I am accused of some bad things but none so *mean* as being a TRAITOR.
>
> Yrs. truly, &c.,
SSR [8]

The February Term of the Grand Jury had continued the cases against Renfroe, and he could do nothing other than wait his August trial. Renfroe and his captors negotiated over the charges he would face, and before the trial an agreement was made. All but two of the various indictments were *nol-prossed.* But to the accusation of grand larceny of a horse, he pleaded guilty and was sentenced to three years. He also pleaded guilty to embezzlement, a confession that condemned him to an addi-

---

[8] Livingston *Journal,* July 30, 1885; see *ibid.,* July 16, 1885.

tional two years. At the age of forty-two Renfroe faced five years in the State penitentiary.[9]

Such a sentence would have been difficult enough in any circumstances, but at the time Alabama practiced the infamous convict "lease" system. As it operated, private individuals or corporations leased the prisoners, employing them in mines, road work, or sawmill camps, and paid the state. The Pratt Coal and Iron Company located near Birmingham (then a burgeoning industrial city of the New South, 127 miles from Livingston) utilized convict labor. The former Sumter County lawman was among the prisoners sent to the coal mines. For a man like Renfroe, going underground every day to work was a consignment to hell. As posed by a Black Belt editor, "The next question is, how long will he remain in the clutches of the law?" [10]

In September 1885, a Birmingham reporter toured the Pratt Mines inspecting facilities and talking with the convicts. His visitation included a call on Renfroe, who seemed glad to see the journalist and gave the impression of having philosophically accepted his degraded environment. He regretted that conditions inhibited his role as host. When advised to make the best of his situation, "He said he would do this, and that as soon as he became accustomed to the work he would have no further troubles, and that just now he felt a little sore from the work he did, but thought he would soon be relieved of this." [11]

That he would be relieved was a reasonable expectation. Renfroe had already planned another escape.

[9] See Record of Cases, Book R, February 25, 1885, 481-482; *ibid.*, August 24, 1885, 594; see also Gainesville *Messenger*, August 29, 1885; Montgomery *Advertiser*, September 1, 1885.

[10] Butler *Choctaw Herald*, September 3, 1885.

[11] Birmingham *Evening Chronicle*, September 19, 1885.

CHAPTER XII

Death at the Sucarnatchie

ccording to one story, Renfroe had agreed to serve his sentence provided he was neither mistreated nor overworked. Otherwise, he promised to "make the best of circumstances." Herr's *Journal* reported that when Renfroe left Livingston he was in no condition to perform hard labor, and added, "it is rumored here that he was whipped several times."[1] Whether this was true or not, he bitterly resented his plight and could not have survived for long working in the mines.

Early Sunday morning, October 3, 1885, Renfroe and three other prisoners (Charles Walker, Norman Morris, and Charles Coleman) escaped—their flight accomplished with professional thoroughness. The details were worked out by Renfroe after he learned one of his conspirators used an auger at his work. Acting on Renfroe's instructions, he removed the auger's handle, placed the instrument in one leg of his pantaloons, and smuggled it into the cell.

On Saturday nights mine officials gave all prisoners their personal clothing, a concession enabling them to take off their stripes for Sunday. Renfroe and his comrades changed clothes and managed to bore out a section of a log during the intervals when the patrolling guard was on the other side of their building. After several hour's labor the job was completed, and the four men went through the opening. Although a guard spotted

[1] Livingston *Semi-Weekly Journal*, October 8, 1885.

them climbing over the stockade wall, they faded swiftly into the night.[2]

Afterwards Renfroe remembered walking six miles to Birmingham, where the fugitives tried but failed to secure a vehicle of some kind. Hoping to elude the bloodhounds they knew would soon be on their trail, the escapees wandered about the streets for awhile, then followed the Alabama Great Southern Railroad into the nearby mountains.[3] After walking about eight miles, the fleeing men believed they had eluded pursuit and stopped to rest. As dawn broke, the barking of bloodhounds interrupted them from taking turns with a razor in the uncomfortable but civilized ritual of shaving. The razor along with some money had been secretly carried into the stockade by Renfroe. When the dogs came into view Coleman separated from the others. Unaccountably, a second prisoner pulled off his shoes and fled alone. Next, Renfroe's remaining companion began to ascend the mountain.

With a sure animal instinct Renfroe raced straight toward the hounds over his old tracks for about fifty yards, and, jumping out to the right, ran down into a clump of trees. He entered a creek and waded down it for about three miles before emerging. Renfroe came out on a mountainside in time to see one of his former comrades captured. Because the hounds had not followed him, Renfroe remained hidden until Monday night when he started down the Alabama Great Southern.[4] Following the track, Renfroe made his way toward Sumter County and the Flat Woods. At Eutaw in Greene County Renfroe encountered a tramp in a hobo jungle, and the two men fell into conversation. Later, as they walked along together the men became less guarded in conversation. Renfroe had not eaten in four days, and half-

---

[2] A. G. Smith, July 17, 1886, to Montgomery *Advertiser;* Livingston *Semi-Weekly Journal,* October 8, 1885. On October 29, 1885, the *Journal* printed an interview between Renfroe and Herr. See also Birmingham *Evening Chronicle,* October 5, 1885.

[3] Interview with Frank Herr, Livingston *Semi-Weekly Journal,* October 29, 1885.

[4] *Ibid.* The Birmingham *Evening Chronicle,* October 5, 1885, mentioned the capture of Morris and Walker. Coleman and Renfroe were still at large.

delirious, revealed his identity. The companions continued on to Livingston, pausing north of town at sundown on Saturday, October 10. Somehow they had obtained some whiskey, and in a drunken stupor Renfroe lay down to sleep. The tramp assured him that he would go into town and get them some food.

Instead of procuring supplies, the vagabond went immediately to Sheriff R. L. McCormick (ironically, McCormick had served as Renfroe's deputy in happier days) and told him where he could find Renfroe. The sheriff quickly summoned a posse to go after the escapee.

Some sense of self-preservation woke Renfroe just as the four-man posse approached. He recounted later that he expected to be killed attempting to escape but preferred anything to returning to the mines. Fortunately for him a moonless night had fallen, so that his huddled form seemed a part of the terrain. The posse, directed to the spot by Renfroe's betrayer, was led by Deputy Robert Barnes. When he got within twenty feet, Renfroe suddenly bolted. Barnes fired at him, missing. Other weapons were discharged, and then Renfroe heard the deputy yell, "Stop, Mc, for God's sake! You've shot me all to pieces."

In the darkness and confusion, Sheriff McCormick had mistaken Barnes for Renfroe and blazed away with his shotgun. By lucky chance the shells were loaded with turkey shot, and although the deputy's back, neck, and head were riddled, the wounds were superficial (although a doctor spent two hours extracting lead from the uncomfortable Barnes). The posse continued its remarkable record of ineptitude by allowing Renfroe to escape completely. No doubt the fugitive was sobered completely by his close call, and, as he reminisced later, he lay hidden the rest of the night.[5]

Two incidents, one near-tragic and the other largely humorous, developed from the abortive attempt to capture Renfroe. W. H. Eastland, his wife, and four children lived within one hundred yards of Renfroe's hastily abandoned refuge. Late that

[5] A. G. Smith, July 17, 1886, to Montgomery *Advertiser;* Herr's interview, Livingston *Semi-Weekly Journal,* October 29, 1885; see also Livingston *Semi-Weekly Journal,* October 11, 1885.

night, at one o'clock, Eastland heard a knock at his door. Thinking it was Renfroe, he ordered his wife to remain in the room, grabbed his 38 Smith & Wesson, and slipped into the hall. After a time his worried wife came out to investigate. The distracted Eastland, thinking she was Renfroe, whirled and fired a shot into her chest. Although her wound was serious, it was not fatal.

As if all this were not excitement enough for one night, at 3:20 in the morning the church bell of the Negro Baptist Church north of town began tolling. A guard was sent scurrying to investigate, and discovered the Negroes holding a solemn prayer meeting! They knew Renfroe had returned. There seemed little doubt that even if Renfroe was a notorious outlaw, he kept the people of Sumter County from becoming bored.

Renfroe's escape set off a controversy that arrayed most of Sumter County against Detective Justus J. Collins of the Pratt Mines. Further, a footnote to the details of Renfroe's flight added to the acrimony. After the wild episodes of Saturday night and Sunday morning, the Pratt Mines sent three detectives to Livingston: Sullivan of Slidell, Louisiana, fame; Collins; and a man named Croswell. They arrived on Monday (October 12), with bloodhounds, but the dogs failed to get a track. Frank Herr, like other Sumter countians familiar with Renfroe's habits, believed the outlaw was still in the neighborhood. Averring that "reckless exposure will nevertheless terminate disasterously sooner or later," Herr tried to calm any feelings of terror by firmly declaring Renfroe did not intend to harm anyone. Yet as a spokeman for the county and in the certain knowledge the escapee would read the article, Herr wrote "if we have any influence with him, we beg him to leave." [6]

Herr was correct: Renfroe was still in the county, hidden deep in the Flat Woods. He wrote a letter to Sheriff McCormick commenting on affairs in general and showing himself knowledgeable of everything in Livingston. Promising to keep its readers informed of new developments, the *Journal* editorialized:

[6] Livingston *Semi-Weekly Journal,* October 15, 1885.

Maybe [Renfroe's] gone up to Birmingham to retaliate on that blood hound party. Who knows? Meanwhile all the fun is not dead here yet. We know of several parties who have been hunting around the public square for him a week. One man wants to support him for Sheriff again. No doubt he'd make a good run if he'd jump into a crowd or two and slash and shoot his pistol around a little. We think of petitioning Cleveland to give him a foreign mission, but its darned doubtful whether he'd accept. It seems this is the only climate that agrees with him. Strange, too! The swamps are full of mosquitoes and the town full of shotguns. But rather than have him laying around idle we'd like to engage him as a contributor to the JOURNAL. He's decidedly the most *pointed* writer we know of.[7]

With Renfroe's past record so well known, with Birmingham detectives scouring the countryside, with frightened Negroes holding prayer meetings, it was to be expected that a sense of disquiet (terror in some quarters) would prevail in Sumter County. To set the citizens' minds at rest, Herr arranged an interview with Renfroe. The rendezvous was set up by specially worded advertisements in the *Journal*. Following directions, an unarmed Herr was met by a gun-carrying sentinel at dusk in a desolate Flat Woods' swamp. The sentinel blew three quick times, sharp and shrill, on an acorn whistle. They waited until they heard a distant reply—one long, faint whistle that seemed to hang in the air. Then the guide whistled again and once more was answered. They began walking and soon a partridge whistle sounded in front. Presently they emerged into a clearing and found Renfroe waiting. He was sitting on a log with a double-barreled breech-loading shotgun on his lap, a large Remington revolver buckled to his waist.

Renfroe, now well fed, described the horrors of the mines, gave the details of his escape, and hoped he could leave before the next mosquito time. He admitted a foreign mission appointment would be tempting. Making clear his temporary residence was not a threat to anyone's safety, Renfroe said he disliked for Sheriff McCormick and the detectives to persist in keeping things stirred up. He emphasized his resolve never to be taken

[7] *Ibid.*, October 18, 1885.

alive. Herr later told his readers Renfroe's well protected hide-out made mass assault impossible. The pursued sheriff, Herr claimed, could pick off his attackers one at a time.

For those interested in how Renfroe used his leisure moments, Herr commented, "He spends most of his time hunting and reading and bags a good deal of nice game—turkeys, partridges, squirrels, &c." The outcast had a good hunting dog whose services included warning his master of approaching danger. "[Renfroe] says its a 'pretty hard life,' but 'beats the coal mines a long way,' and that he never intends to go back." [8]

If Herr's published interview caused relief in Sumter County, it had the opposite effect in Birmingham. An infuriated Detective Collins wrote a letter of reply to Frank Herr. Collins vowed to catch Renfroe eventually, decrying what he considered an attempt to make Renfroe a hero. "No one need have any doubt about his capture some day—and I intend to make every body smoke who has had anything to do with aiding him if I can get evidence to convict."

How, Collins wondered, had Renfroe secured arms, to say nothing of a sentinel? Collins said Renfoe went to Birmingham after his escape looking, unsuccessfully as it turned out, for the home of a Miss Lou Wooster, "a woman of bad repute." His purpose was to get a gun left there for him by Walter H. Wilson. A former guard at the Pratt Mines, Wilson had arranged to steal a gun for Renfroe and leave it at Miss Wooster's residence. The design failed when the gun was missed by company authorities and the exposed Wilson was forced to flee. Renfroe, unaware of Wilson's difficulties, allegedly wasted his time seeking the woman's house.

Collins was also critical of Sumter County because he believed the citizens there were protecting and providing for Renfroe. Speaking for the other detectives, Collins wrote, "We are very much relieved to learn through the medium of your valuable paper that Renfroe will not molest us, if we manage to keep out of his way." [9] Collins' criticisms brought retorts from two

[8] *Ibid.*, October 29, 1885.
[9] Birmingham *Evening Chronicle*, November 9, 1885.

sources. Herr denied that Sumter County was sheltering Renfroe. It was not the county's fault that a guard helped him escape. As for Renfroe's companion in the Flat Woods, Herr could not identify him.[10]

Miss Lou Wooster, a resolute woman, went to the office of the Birmingham *Evening Chronicle* to correct what she considered malicious statements. She said that Wilson told her Renfroe, whom she had known earlier, needed food and that she sent him some. The food would have been sent, she insisted, even if Renfroe had been a stranger. Wilson also asked permission to leave a gun at her house. She consented but knew nothing of any conspiracy. Later Wilson and another man came to claim the weapon. Beyond these facts she had no knowledge of the escape from the Pratt Mines. "When I knew Renfroe," she declared, "he was a gentleman whose character was above reproach, and I never saw him after he was accused of crime."

If Collins' anger at being thwarted was understandable, so too were the reactions of the people of Sumter County and Miss Wooster.[11]

Still unable to leave the area, Renfroe remained hidden in the Flat Woods, moving back and forth from Alabama to Mississippi. Newspapers reported he had joined a band of horse thieves. One writer claimed he took from Sumter County "no less than ten mules and horses." [12] These and other stories depicting him as a savage master criminal were exaggerated. The truth was more harsh as the collapse of Renfroe's life became unmistakable.

As October faded into November, Renfroe began to feel the autumn chill that sometimes comes suddenly in Alabama. One sees him huddled miserably around a wet fire, glancing overhead at a deceptive sun that contained no warmth. On Christmas Eve Renfroe could stand the isolation no longer. Desperately seeking companionship of some kind, he went to Meridian. He sent a note to the *Times-Democrat* offering that paper an interview provided he would not be betrayed. The necessary promises and arrangements were made. The reporter who met him was

10 Livingston *Semi-Weekly Journal,* November 5, 1885.
11 Birmingham *Evening Chronicle,* November 10, 1885.
12 Montgomery *Advertiser,* July 14, 1886.

shocked at Renfroe's condition—his health was broken, his swagger gone, the coal black hair streaked with grey. Renfroe said he was passing through Meridian on his way to Mexico. Money and supplies for his exodus had been furnished by his friends. When he left that night the interviewer was only partly persuaded that Sumter County "is perhaps at last rid of a man who has lived within its bounds in open defiance of the law for several years." [13]

But, trapped by circumstances and accumulated experience, Renfroe was incapable of leaving Sumter County. Operating out of the Flat Woods he was seen or reported seen in the region throughout the first half of 1886. In May he supposedly passed through Grove Hill in Clarke County seated on a stolen saddle girted around a stolen horse, armed with a stolen gun. Pursuit was organized, but the rider, if Renfroe, was never overtaken. Closer home, in June a horse belonging to E. W. Hooks was stolen from a livery stable at York. The automatic assumption was that Renfroe had struck again.

Shortly afterwards, the county was alerted when the home of Mrs. M. S. Harris, a Livingston widow who had frequently befriended the outlaw, was entered and robbed of silver plate valued at $250. In the interval between the thefts at York and Livingston a man answering Renfroe's description was seen in the county. Then on the night of July 7, E. S. "Sim" Sledge, a former brother-in-law of Renfroe's who lived eight miles west of Livingston, had a fine mule stolen.[14]

Each new act added to the outlaw's notoriety and upped the reward for his capture. In February Governor E. A. O'Neal had raised the bounty on Renfroe to $400. The Pratt Mines had an offer of $100 still unclaimed, and now the unfortunate Sledge put up $50, bringing to $550 the reward for Renfroe's capture.[15]

While the thefts were taking place, a man was seen by several persons passing at fairly regular intervals from Alabama toward Enterprise, a small town about fifteen miles south of

[13] Interview quoted in Talladega *Our Mountain Home*, December 30, 1885.

[14] Montgomery *Advertiser*, July 15, 1886.

[15] Governor's Proclamations 1882-1898, 87; Birmingham *Evening Chronicle*, October 5, 1885.

Meridian in Clarke County, Mississippi. The unidentified man always seemed to ride a different horse or mule and stop invariably at the house of a Negro near Enterprise. Interested persons approached the Negro who admitted entertaining a white man from time to time but denied knowing his name. The Negro promised to inform the men the next time the stranger stopped off. On Saturday July 10, Renfroe rode up to the Negro cabin on a healthly young mule. Pausing only briefly, he rode west toward Smith County. After the visit the Negro informed three men—W. P. H. Ainsworth, S. R. Hinton, and Sim Windham—of Renfroe's departure, and the trio started in pursuit.

Accounts of the capture by the three farmers vary but not in any significant details. They caught up with Renfroe on Sunday afternoon at one o'clock. Apparently they had circled ahead of him and lay in wait. The unsuspecting fugitive was riding casually along with an umbrella in his hand when they ordered him to halt. He glanced up, suddenly attentive, but before he could draw his Navy Six, one of the men sighted down the barrel of a shotgun and sent a load of bird shot smashing into Renfroe's side and back. The mule, also shot, bolted, throwing Renfroe to the ground. The captive was not seriously injured. After he identified himself as "John Jones," Renfroe was searched: his possessions were limited to a clothes brush, a razor and shaving soap, a receipt for a shotgun from a New Orleans pawnshop, and a picture of his twelve-year-old son (the boy's face was one of "exceeding brightness").

The prisoner was brought back to Enterprise, where Thomas George, a former resident of Sumter County, positively identified him as Renfroe. For some reason no doctor was summoned. But despite a shotgun wound and the debilitating effects of several months of hiding, Renfroe's powerful constitution kept him functioning. The men who brought him in, represented by James S. Boyd, sent telegrams on Monday morning, July 12, to Livingston and Birmingham establishing their claim to the reward money.[16]

---

[16] See Mobile *Register*, July 15, 1886; Montgomery *Advertiser*, July 15, 1886; Birmingham *Iron Age*, July 15, 1886; Livingston *Journal*, July 22, 1886.

Detective Collins, who seemed to have been contacted by Ainsworth, made preparations to arrest Renfroe for the Pratt Mines. At Livingston Dr. W. H. Sledge, brother of the "Sim" Sledge whose mule was stolen, received word that both the mule and the widow Harris' silverware had been located. He replied by telegram: "Guard Renfroe regardless of cost; will be after him to-night." With a warrant charging Renfroe with grand larceny, Dr. Sledge, Sheriff McCormick, and Steve Smith left Livingston by train. They were less than pleased to discover Detective Collins also on board. A dispute immediately arose over who had proper authority to make the arrest.

When the train stopped at Meridian, Collins sent a hurried telegram to Ainsworth: "Your reward is in danger. Also have heard news of lynching Renfroe at Livingston. A crowd on train from that place. Slip him on South bound M. &. O. [Mobile & Ohio] freight, off side of the cars and go to Mobile with me." When Ainsworth and his worried associates received Collins' message they took Renfroe to a river bank outside of town, bound him, and stood guard. The Livingston party was unable to find Renfroe when they arrived at Enterprise. Not until Boyd recognized Dr. Sledge and supposedly remarked, "Boys, this is all right," was Renfroe brought out of hiding to the town's only hotel and imprisoned in a small room. There negotiations began between Boyd and two of the captors and the Livingston group. Evidently Collins waited outside, three hundred yards away at the depot. He claimed he was making an agreement with Hinton to take charge of the prisoner.

Back at the hotel a new problem arose. Hugh Wilson, a Mississippi lawman, forced his way into the already crowded room displaying yet another warrant for Renfroe. It seemed that Renfroe had stolen a mule from a certain Rosenbaum of Lauderdale County. The matter was compromised when the Alabama officers paid Wilson $25.

After Wilson left, Collins entered the room in time to see the captors attempt to put handcuffs on Renfroe. He resisted violently, and in the struggle the handcuffs became locked and could not be reopened. Collins' offer of his own handcuffs was accepted. Assisted by Boyd, he placed them on a suddenly docile Renfroe. "I then concluded," Collins was to write, "I had the possession absolutely of him, in accordance with the agreement made with Hinton for himself and the other two captors." Collins based his primary claim on Renfroe's status as an escaped convict. McCormick and the others said Renfroe had already been surrendered to them and arrangements made to return him to Livingston. The Sumter County men paid Renfroe's fare to Livingston. (Collins said he also paid it.)

From Enterprise to the Alabama state line Collins made no further attempts to take charge of the prisoner. In the rush to leave Livingston, Sheriff McCormick had forgotten to bring the warrant that would make the arrest legal. Fortunately for him, W. B. Edmundson, a Sumter County justice who happened to be on the train, consented to issue a warrant, and the document was delivered by McCormick at the state boundary. Once in Alabama, Collins renewed his maneuvers. His demand for Renfroe was refused. At one point when the sheriff was in another car, Collins made an attempt to place shackles on Renfroe's legs. Dr. Sledge forbade him to do this. Backing up his statement, the physician placed a shell into his gun and snapped the barrel into place.

Collins believed the prisoner had been taken from him by force and protested Renfroe's being taken off the train at Livingston. McCormick and the others countered with the claim that they were legally entitled to Renfroe, had arrested him with proper papers, and were carrying out the desires of his captors who wanted Renfroe lodged in the first available jail. It is difficult to say who had the better claim, although Boyd later wrote a letter stating he definitely turned Renfroe over to Sheriff Mc-Cormick.[17]

The train bearing Renfroe arrived at Livingston at 5:20 Tuesday morning, July 13. A large crowd waited at the station despite the early hour. As the day progressed the throng swelled as people gathered from all parts of the county. One observer wrote, "To hang Renfroe was determined upon by everybody

---

[17] *Ibid.* For Boyd's letter to Steve Smith see Gainesville *Messenger*, August 13, 1886.

without even any special understanding about it. . . ." Another reporter predicted, "It is not unlikely that an outraged community may deal summarily with the outlaw." Seeing the faces, most of them familiar, Renfroe exclaimed, "It is Katy with me." [18]

It seems probable Renfroe would have been hanged immediately, but the people felt obligated to wait for Jim Boyd to collect the reward. Collins signed the bounty papers for the Mississippians, insisting, however, that Renfroe was his prisoner. The detective exhibited a dispatch which purported to be from the attorney general of the state. When that official sided with Collins, a convinced Sheriff McCormick agreed to deliver Renfroe to the detective. The sheriff advised Collins to take the prisoner to Brimingham on the 8:22 train that night. Apparently McCormick and several other men in Livingston offered to go with them as far as the Greene County line.

During the day a number of citizens went down to visit Renfroe in jail, although they found him in no mood to communicate. But as the morning passed into afternoon and dusk approached, Renfroe asked for an interview with Frank Herr. The editor entered his cell about five o'clock.

Speaking without emotion, Renfroe said he knew he was to be hanged and did not want the sixty-odd bird shot removed from his back. He regretted that the farmers had not killed him instead of taking him prisoner. He did not wish to continue his present way of life but realized there was no way to lead any other—he only wanted the end to come as soon as possible and preferably by shooting instead of hanging, although he would not beg. Again he blamed his troubles on whiskey. He recalled as a youth his ambition to become famous, lamenting death by the hangman's knot instead of death as a hero fighting enemies. Renfroe kept insisting that he desired no special consideration, but he did ask that his wife change the last name of his son.[19]

In July night falls slowly. After the excitement of the day the evening was quiet, the air warm and languid. Many citizens

[18] Mobile *Register*, July 16, 1886, quoting Meridian *News;* Birmingham *Iron Age*, July 15, 1886.

[19] Livingston *Journal*, July 22, 1886; Birmingham *Weekly Iron Age*, July 29, 1886; Herr, "Reconstruciton in Sumter County," 8.

were either at supper or had finished eating and were sitting out on their front porches talking and watching the moon come up. The outer jail door was not yet closed for the night when a party of eight men appeared before the building. Two of them entered Jailor Clark's room. They seized him, took his cell keys, and, pistols drawn, told the jailor if he gave the alarm they would kill him. While the two men guarded Clark, the others took possession of Renfroe, and the party moved off.

There was no mob—the intent not to have one was deliberate. The very boldness of the scheme contributed to its success. It was just 8:30. The men formed a procession with Renfroe in the center and marched through the lower part of Livingston, passing within a few feet of various citizens (many of them recognized Renfroe, for it was understood that no less than seventy-five men were ready to help if needed). Incredible as it seems, the somber group of men attracted little notice. No one was disguised. Not a word was spoken.[20] The men passed by the home of Miss "Tempie" Scruggs; she and her sister—then young girls— were seated on their front porch, hidden by the bannister. Drawing from the never-forgotten memories of that night Miss "Tempie" recalled:

> It was a beautiful moon-light night. You could see as plain as in day-light. We saw them coming from way up the street, men marching two by two with hardly a sound except what sounded like the clink of a chain. The men wore dusters and hats pulled down. We knew something terrible was going to happen, and we dropped down on the porch and watched them through the railing. They were so quiet.[21]

The procession halted just south of town near an old tanyard on the banks of the Sucarnatchie River. There at a broad bend, where Moylan's cavalry used to camp, stood a chinaberry tree— its bark grey-black and its limbs heavy with dark green leaves. The men led Renfroe under this tree. He moved unbowed in a detached gait. At some point during this last capture, a sub-

---

[20] Birmingham *Weekly Iron Age*, July 29, 1886, has important letters from Collins and McCormick, Smith, and Sledge stating their positions.

[21] Authors' interview June 1964, with Mrs. Temple Ennis, of Livingston.

missive resignation had wrapped itself around him. Only one trace of the old Renfroe manifested itself—despite the degraded circumstances he died with quiet dignity.

Renfroe displayed no fear when a rope was placed around his neck. When the other end was thrown over a tree limb, one of the party asked if he wanted to pray. Renfroe said, "Boys, you know I have never prayed in my life." Did he want someone to pray for him? "If anyone wants to," he answered. One of his executioners stepped forward in the soft moonlight, raised his hands above Renfroe's pale face and, glancing heavenward, intoned, "God have mercy upon the soul of this miserable man."

Renfroe, statuesque and without outcry, was pulled clear of the ground and the rope made fast to another tree. Attached to his back was a placard that read, "The fate of a horse thief." [22]

Jailor Clark did not delay long in spreading the alarm. He raced to find Sheriff McCormick and a posse was quickly raised. But it was too late. When the pursuers reached the Sucarnatchie they saw the grim spectacle. The corpse was cut down and brought back to town.

The Livingston *Journal* reported, "We understand that, while those of the party seen by the jailor were not disguised, he did not recognize any of them." That he did recognize them seems certain, and, for that matter, the particulars of the hanging and the participants were known to a large number of people. No action was ever taken against them. A seven man jury of inquest, called by Squire Robert Tankersley, declared: "We the Jury of Inquest summoned to examine into the cause of death of S. S. Renfroe, having examined the evidence state that said Renfroe came to his death by hanging; which hanging was done by persons unknown." [23]

---

[22] Birmingham *Evening Chronicle*, July 14, 1886; Montgomery *Daily Dispatch*, October 10, 1886; Mobile *Register*, July 16, 1886, quoting Meridian *News;* Livingston *Journal*, July 22, 1886; Gainesville *Messenger*, July 16, 1886; Herr, "Reconstruction in Sumter County," 8-11. One version of the hanging had Renfroe replying when asked if he had anything to say, "Not a damned thing, except that I would rather be in hell than the Alabama coal mines."

[23] Livingston *Journal*, July 22, 1886.

Renfroe's body was placed on a prison cot in the open hallway of the courthouse, and he lay alone on the threshhold of the sheriff's office he had once occupied. No candle was lit, no sound was heard. Tree limbs partially blocked out the moonlight and cast shadows along the courthouse corridor and across Renfroe's body.

The family did not receive Renfroe's corpse. There were no mourners. There was no burial in the town cemetery, not even a funeral service. Stephen S. Renfroe received a pauper's burial in a potter's field. His final resting place was an unmarked grave.[24]

[24] Herr, "Reconstruction in Sumter County," 12.

CHAPTER XIII

Aftermath

Despite the finality of the hanging, Renfroe stirred controversy in death as he had in life. Beyond the Atlanta *Constitution's* remark that Renfroe "was well educated and desperate," or the Chicago *Times'* similar assertion, there was a discordant outpouring of opinion.[1] Whether lynching the outlaw sheriff had served the best interests of justice became the principal issue.

The Montgomery *Advertiser* took an unequivocal position: "Society is in danger when men make a law unto themselves and undertake to do acts of violence under the plea of providing for future safety." Moreover, "Ever if RENFROE was a terror to the community there is no justification for men riding over law and courts and taking life where the law made no such demand."[2] Seconding this position, the Greensboro *Alabama Beacon* believed "However bad a man Renfroe was, it would have been better that he should have been tried and punished legally." The *Beacon* declared emphatically, "Mob law, under any state of circumstances, is dangerous, and should, when it is possible, be avoided."[3]

Other newspapers found justification for the act. "There are times and cases where Lynch Law is justifiable, and no man can

---

[1] July 14, 1886; see Chicago *Times*, July 14, 1886.

[2] July 15, 1886.

[3] July 20, 1886. The Greensboro *Watchman* was also critical of the lynching.

deny that Renfroe [merited] his doom," the Gainesville *Messenger* analyzed. "Like most well bred men," a Troy paper editorialized, "he went rapidly to indulgence in excesses of crime which deserved the death penalty." [4] One sophistical correspondent wrote that in view of Renfroe's record, "No one can regret his taking off." [5]

The Livingston *Journal* assumed the major burden of defending the extreme extra-legal action. When Renfroe was at large, the *Journal* pointed out, the citizens of Sumter County were criticized for permitting a desperado to terrorize the community; when he escaped from the Pratt Mines, they were charged with harboring an outlaw; and now that he had been hanged, the people were accused of tarnishing the state's reputation. "Verily the people of Sumter have had exacting masters."

The paper listed the many crimes charged to Renfroe and mentioned several others which had not resulted in indictments but which by common agreement were committed by the deceased sheriff. "This community felt a relief they had not enjoyed for years" when Renfroe was sentenced to prison for five years. But in less than sixty days he had escaped to the Flat Woods, a vantage spot that enabled him to make forays on the county at his pleasure and with impunity—the outlaw had "trusty negro spies and watchers who served him with fidelity."

Editor Herr correctly observed that in the final days Renfroe seemed depraved, treating former friends and foes alike. If Sumter County officials had been unable to capture Renfroe, so too had the detectives of the Pratt Mines, the editor added. Neither Herr nor the people of Sumter County made any effort to glorify or even defend mob violence. That such action was illegal and reprehensible they agreed. What they attempted was an explanation (or perhaps a rationalization) of why it had occurred. The primary reason Renfroe was hanged, in Herr's opinion, was the "apprenhension that the protection of the community could not otherwise be assured." If the fugitive had been

---

[4] July 16, 1886; Troy *Enquirer*, July 17, 1886.

[5] Sumter County correspondent to Montgomery *Advertiser*, July 14, 1886.

merely returned to the Pratt Mines, it was highly likely he would have escaped again. Because he seemed to have lost all control over his actions, Renfroe would have become more dangerous than ever. In brief, his return to prison "afforded no assurance of protection against his lawlessness." [6]

Yet some asserted strongly that Renfroe did not deserve to be hanged. He was serving a five-year sentence and had not been convicted of any crime punishable by death. His actions were wild and his health broken, but his bravery when facing death, his determination to spare his son the stigma of the name Renfroe—were these the acts of a demented and wanton murderer?

The New York *World* hinted darkly at unmentioned motives for the hanging: "It is gravely suspected that Renfroe was put out of the way for what he could tell more than what he had done, for since Ku-Klux times he had not done anything that the law could hang him for." [7] Identical explanations were advanced by local people and still persist. Renfroe, according to this thesis, knew who the Klan members were and had either threatened to expose them or they were afraid he would. Before he could compromise the image of several respectable citizens, he was eliminated. While this theory is possible, it seems unlikely. Renfroe could have made public the names of Klan members on any number of occasions had he chosen. Even had he done so in 1886, there was no indignant public crusade to bring former Klansmen to justice. Besides, at that point Renfroe's word would scarely have been considered reliable.

Regardless of how they reacted to the disgraced man's death, newspapers and other commentators recognized something special in Renfroe. "Thus died Steve Renfroe, an able man, who by his courage and indominable [*sic*] will, might have been eminent for good in this world," the Greenville *Advocate* lamented.[8] One writer remembered: "A Confederate soldier, [Renfroe] won the love of his comrades—a rescuer of Sumter County from Radical rule, he merited the respect of her best

[6] July 29, 1886.
[7] July 15, 1886.
[8] July 21, 1886.

citizens—a true Democrat, he won the confidence of the party, and was rewarded for his fidelity." In massive understatement and summation the Troy *Enquirer* agreed, "He led a remarkably strange and eventful career. . . ."[9]

So Renfroe died and his legend began. The people of the Black Belt, whites and Negroes, told stories of his prowess for generations. According to legend, Renfroe's spirit, dressed in billowing white robes and riding a white horse named Death, returned every July 13, to the spot of his hanging. As the rider and his mount descended, the sky turned green; the leaves on the chinaberry tree rustled without benefit of a breeze; and the waters of the Sucarnatchie suddenly rippled into mild turbulence—a warning to the wayward. Then Death, spurred by his phantom rider, would gallop upward again, and those brave enough to witness the scene could observe the ethereal figures disappear into the summer sky.

Local people claimed cattle would not seek the shade of the hanging tree; nor would birds build their nests in its branches. They declared that grass never grew beneath its limbs. The death tree, they said, was the first to shed its leaves in the fall and the last to put forth in the spring.

There were those who swore that in the darkest hours of night, in the dead of winter, the bugle notes of Moylan's cavalry—gone years ago with Custer—sounded a ghostly anthem to their unit and to Renfroe. For years Negro and white youths refused to go near the place of Renfroe's death after dark. Just the thought of Renfroe was enough to drive a boy out of bed on a winter night and send him scurrying barefoot across a cold floor to make sure the door was locked.[10]

Renfroe's wife and son moved to another city, where he assumed another name. As for Renfroe, missing parts of his story may be found in time, although a complete biography probably cannot be written. Although he can be placed in historical perspective, why he acted as he did will always remain a matter of interpretation or reasoned guesses. Shortly after he was hanged,

[9] Gainesville *Messenger*, July 16, 1886; Troy *Enquirer*, July 17, 1886.
[10] Herr, "Reconstruction in Sumter County," 10-11.

Renfroe received attention from a Mobile editor. The journalist's words were not adequate to explain an entire life, but there was considerable truth to his conclusion: "It was Steve Renfroe's destiny to be hanged some day, and his destiny has simply been accomplished sooner than was expected." [11]

Today, Livingston's courthouse square, still shaded by large oaks, remains about the same as it was in the days of Renfroe. The bored well is still there, and the tax rolls in the red-brick courthouse are embossed with names common to Sumter County for generations. If one, whose curiosity led him to an exploration of a bygone era, should enter the Records Room of the courthouse and ask for Docket Book S, the Clerk would bring out a leatherbound volume. On page 68 he would find the record of two cases, The State vs Stephen S. Renfroe, and opposite the indictments are the words:

"Abated by death of defendant."[12]

[11] Mobile *Register*, July 15, 1886.
[12] Record of Cases, Book S, August 1886, 68.

Bibliography

PRIMARY SOURCES

Documents

Alabama *Acts*, 1868.

Eighth Census of the United States, 1860.

Select Committee on Affairs in Alabama, 43 Cong., 2 Sess., No. 262. Washington: Government Printing Office, 1875.

Testimony Taken by the Joint Select Committee to Inquire Into the Condition of Affairs in the Late Insurrectionary States. 42 Cong., 2 sess. No. 22, 13 vols. Washington: Government Printing Office, 1872.

Manuscripts

Butler County Marriage Licenses 1865-1868, Butler County Courthouse, Greenville, Alabama.

Census Returns 1860, Butler County, Department of Archives and History, Montgomery, Alabama.

Census Returns 1870, 1880, Sumter County, Department of Archives and History.

Correspondence of Governor David P. Lewis, Department of Archives and History.

Correspondence of Governor William H. Smith, Department of Archives and History.

Correspondence of Wager Swayne, Department of Archives and History.

Freedmen's Bureau Files, Department of Archives and History.

Freedmen's Bureau Records for Alabama, National Archives, Washington, D.C.

Governor's Proclamation Book, December 24, 1860, to December 26, 1881, Book G, Department of Archives and History.

Lauderdale County Marriage Records, December 25, 1867, to January 4, 1879, Book 1-A, Lauderdale County Courthouse, Meridian, Mississippi.

Letterbook of Stephen S. Renfroe, Sumter County Courthouse, Livingston, Alabama.

Military Posts 1800-1916, United States Returns, Roll 638, National Archives, Washington, D.C.

NA Publications, Microcopy 666 Rolls 169-173, RG 94, National Archives.

Original Roll, Company G, Ninth Alabama Infantry Regiment, Department of Archives and History.

Record Cases, Books R, S, and U, 1880, 1881, 1885, Sumter County Courthouse.

Sumter County Deed Books, T, 1870; 2, 1878; 10 and 11, 1880, Sumter County Courthouse.

Sumter County Marriage Records, 1864-1873, Department of Archives and History.

Newspapers

Atlanta *Constitution*, 1886.

Birmingham *Evening Chronicle*, 1885.

Birmingham *Iron Age*, 1886.

Butler *Choctaw Herald*, 1874, 1884-1885.

Chicago *Inter Ocean*, 1874-1875.

Chicago *Times*, 1886.

Eutaw *Whig and Observer*, 1884.

Florence *Republican*, 1874.

Gainesville *Messenger,* 1885-1886.

Gainesville *News,* 1868-1871.

Greensboro *Alabama Beacon,* 1886.

Greenville *Advocate,* 1867, 1874.

Jackson [Mississippi] *Weekly Clarion,* 1871.

Linden *Reporter,* 1882.

Livingston *Journal,* 1867-1868, 1871-1875, 1878, 1880, 1882, 1885-1886.

Livingston *Messenger,* 1867.

Montgomery *Advertiser,* 1878, 1885-1886.

Montgomery *Alabama State Journal,* 1868, 1874.

Montgomery *Daily Dispatch,* 1886.

Montgomery *Daily Mail,* 1867.

New Orleans *Daily Picayune,* 1874.

New York *Daily Tribune,* 1871.

New York *Times,* 1874.

New York *World,* 1886.

Talladega *Our Mountain Home,* 1885.

Tallahassee *Weekly Floridian,* 1886.

Troy *Enquirer,* 1886.

Tuscaloosa *Gazette,* 1883-1884.

Tuscaloosa *Blade,* 1874.

SECONDARY SOURCES
Books

Chalmers, David M., *Hooded Americanism: The First Century of the Ku Klux Klan, 1865-1965.* Garden City, New York: Doubleday, 1965.

Damer, Syre, *When the Ku Klux Klan Rode.* New York: Neale Publishing Company, 1912.

DuBose, John Witherspoon, *Alabama's Tragic Decade.* Birmingham: Webb Book Company, 1940.

Fleming, Walter L., *Civil War and Reconstruction in Alabama.* Chicago: S. J. Clarke Publishing Co., 1906.

Garner, James Wilford, *Reconstruction in Mississippi*. New York: Macmillan, 1901.

Horn, Stanley F., *Invisible Empire: The Story of the Ku Klux Klan, 1866-1871*. Boston: Houghton Mifflin, 1939.

Jenkins, Nelle Morris, *Pioneer Families of Sumter County, Alabama*. Tuscaloosa: Willo Publishing Company, 1961.

Randel, William Pierce, *The Ku Klux Klan: A Century of Infamy*. Philadelphia: Chilton Books, 1965.

Sellers, James Benson, *Slavery in Alabama*. University: University of Alabama Press, 1950.

Semmes, Raphael, *Serivce Afloat; Or, The Remarkable Career of the Confederate Cruisers Sumter and Alabama. . . .* Baltimore: Kelly, Piet & Co., 1869.

Spratt, R. D., *History of the Town of Livingston, Alabama*. n.p., 1928.

Somers, Robert, *The Southern States Since the War 1870-71*. Introduction by Malcolm C. McMillan. University: University of Alabama Press, 1965.

Articles and Theses

Dillard, Anthony Winston, "History of Sumter County," reprinted in 1869 in the Gainesville *News;* typed copy on file at the Sumter County Courthouse.

Herr, Frank, "Incidents of Reconstruction Days; Sumter County Alabama Following the Civil War." On file at the Sumter County Courthouse.

McGehee, Katharine Louise, "The Meridian Race Riot of 1871," unpublished Honors Thesis, Florida State University, Tallahassee, 1966.

Shank, George K., Jr., "Meridian: A Mississippi City at Birth, During the Civil War, and in Reconstruction," *Journal of Mississippi History*, XXVI (November, 1964), 275-182.

Sloan, John Z., "The Ku Klux Klan and the Alabama Election of 1872," *Alabama Review*, XVII (April, 1965), 113-123.

Taylor, James Leroy, "History of the Ku Klux Klan in Alabama 1865-1874," unpublished Master's Thesis, Auburn University, 1957.

Weisberger, Bernard A., "The Dark and Bloody Ground of Reconstruction Historiography," *Journal of Southern History,* XXVI (November, 1959), 427-447.

Williamson, Edward W., "The Alabama Election of 1874," *Alabama Review,* XVII (July, 1964), 210-218.

Woolfolk, Sarah Van V., "Carpetbaggers in Alabama: Tradition Versus Truth," *Alabama Review,* XV (April, 1962), 133-144.

Index